ESSENTIAL
HEALTH FOR
WOMEN

ESSENTIAL
HEALTH FOR
WOMEN

SHARON WALKER

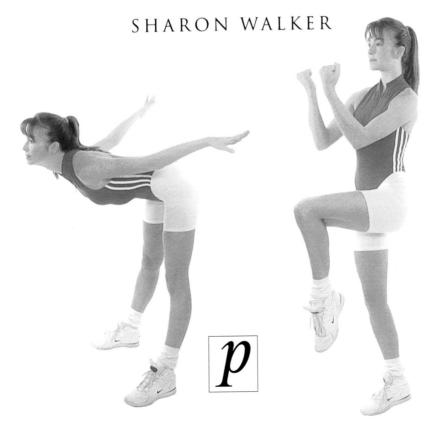

p

This is a Parragon Book
This edition published in 2001

Parragon
Queen Street House
4 Queen Street
Bath BA1 1HE, UK

Copyright © Parragon 1999

Designed, produced and packaged by
Stonecastle Graphics Ltd
Old Chapel Studio, Plain Road, Marden,
Tonbridge, Kent TN12 9LS, United Kingdom

ISBN 0-75256-461-7

Printed in Spain

Photographic credits:

*(Abbreviations: r = right, l = left, t = top, b = below
c = centre)*

The publishers would like to thank the
following for permission to reproduce their
photographs:

Telegraph Colour Library: 8(*r*), 15(*l*); 17(*t*),
17(*l*), 18, 19(*tc*), 19(*tr*), 20(*t*), 22(*t*), 24, 25(*tl*),
25(*bl*), 28(*t*), 30, 32, 33(*tl*), 33(*c*), 33(*bl*), 39(*bl*),
43(*t*), 43(*bc*), 44(*b*), 45(*r*), 47(*b*), 50, 51, 53(*t*),
55(*t*), 56, 57, 58, 59(*bl*), 59(*bc*), 60, 61(*tc*), 63,
65(*br*), 67(*b*), 69(*tl*), 69(*tc*), 69(*bl*), 70, 71, 74(*r*),
75(*bl*), 75(*tr*), 75(*rc*), 77(*bl*), 79 (*b*), 86, 91(*tr*),
93(*tl*), 93(*tr*).

The Image Bank: 31(*bl*), 41(*bl*), 54, 90.

Touchstone: 6(*l*), 6-7(*t*), 7(*l*), 8(*l*), 9, 10, 11(*b*),
12, 13(*t*), 14, 15(*r*), 16, 19, 20(*b*), 21, 23(*tl*),
23(*tr*), 26(*l*), 27(*r*), 28(*b*), 29(*bl*), 59(*t*), 61(*tr*),
61(*br*), 65(*tr*), 69(*tr*), 69(*rc*), 69(*br*), 73(*tl*), 73(*br*),
85, 89(*l*), 91(*b*), 93(*b*), 95(*bl*).

All other pictures © Parragon Publishing
With thanks to Pinpoint Photography and
Peter Pugh-Cook for all commissioned
photographs.

Contents

Health in Our Hands
6

Eating for Health and Vitality
8

Eat Plants to Live
12

Sensible Slimming
16

Healthy Meal Planning
20

Eating to Prevent Osteoporosis
22

Eating for Pregnancy
24

Superfood Supplements
26

Food Allergies
28

Coping with Stress
30

Exercise for Body and Mind
32

Weight Training
34

Aerobic Exercise
36

Walk Yourself Fit
38

Run for Your Life
40

Pedal Power
42

Swimming
44

Step and Aerobics
46

Using a Gym
48

Adolescence
50

Contraception
52

Sexual Health
56

Perfect Pregnancy
58

The Menopause
60

A Good Night's Sleep
62

Eating Disorders
64

Looking After Your Breasts
66

Healthy Hair
68

Skin Care
70

Hands and Nails
72

Teeth / Bright-Eyes
74 / 75

Amazing Feet
76

Massage for Relaxation
78

Aromatherapy
80

Yoga
82

Homeopathy
84

Reflexology
86

Back to Basics
88

Acupuncture
90

Manipulative Therapies
92

Herbal Remedies
94

Index
96

Health in Our Hands

Good health is one of the most precious gifts we can give ourselves. There is now a mountain of evidence to suggest that the lifestyle choices we make will affect our health in later life. Yet sadly we often choose to do nothing, partly because we are too busy and partly because we are not sure what we can do.

The media encourage us to believe that glowing health is the prerogative of celebrities with personal trainers and personal dieticians. What's more, when we do switch from butter to margarine to try to be healthy, the next thing we know the experts have changed their minds. It's too hard to keep up with the rapidly changing recommendations, so we ignore them instead.

Looking after your health now is an insurance policy for later life and more than ever before, women need to take care of their health. Illnesses such as heart disease, ulcers, cirrhosis of the liver and cancers of the throat, lungs and pancreas were traditionally thought of as men's ailments, but a worrying pattern is emerging in modern medicine: women are becoming more like men.

▽ *A colourful and healthy fresh fruit salad.*

Women have stressful jobs and they are smoking and drinking more. Heart disease now kills as many women under 65 as breast cancer and cervical cancer combined. But what can we do to stop it?

Reducing the risks

A high-fat diet, stress, smoking and lack of exercise are all known risk factors in heart disease and many other fatal illnesses. But knowing what we should do is one thing and putting it into practice is something else altogether. We all know we should eat a healthy diet, but we also want to enjoy our food. We know we should exercise, but we haven't got time to spend hours at the gym. We know we should give up cigarettes, but we still reach for one when we're under stress.

The good news is that a little bit of alcohol can do us good; a healthy diet can be just as delicious as an unhealthy one and you don't even have to join a gym to get fit.

This book is for every woman who wants to maximize her health, but who hasn't got the time or the money to spend on dieticians and personal trainers. It's full of practical things you can do to

improve your health without giving up all the pleasures in your life.

It doesn't recommend that you eat nothing but vegetables and brown rice, or get up every day at 6am to go jogging. How much you do is up to you. Remember small changes that last a lifetime count more than a diet or exercise programme you can't stick to for more than a week.

▷ A sensible diet full of fresh foods and regular exercise will improve general health and reward you with healthy skin, shining hair and bright eyes.

Eating for Health and Vitality

What we eat is a fundamental cornerstone of our health. Scientists studying the incidence of disease now believe you can reduce your risk of cancer by two thirds if you cut out smoking and eat healthily.

Never before have dieticians and medical experts known so much about good nutrition, yet ironically, it's never been so difficult to eat a healthy diet. Sweets, chocolates and ready-prepared convenience foods were once considered a luxury, but are now the norm. The average woman consumes 13 teaspoons of sugar daily – that's 265 calories with little nutritional value.

Sadly there's more profit in highly processed foods than natural, wholesome ingredients like fruit and vegetables. And millions are spent on advertising to boost junk food sales. Yet all the evidence suggests that the more processed foods we eat, the less healthy our diet. The trouble is, processed foods tend to be high in sugar, fat, and salt to make them tasty – and these are the specific things we should be cutting back on.

Guidelines for a healthy diet

Remember eating well isn't just about cutting back. Eating for a healthy life is about having more, not less, of certain foods. A healthy diet means enjoying delicious meals, not weighing out tiny portions and counting calories.

Dieticians generally recommend that at least 60 per cent of our energy should come from carbohydrates like fruit, vegetables, bread, potatoes and rice; 20–30 per cent from fat-like oils and butter and 10–20 per cent from protein such as nuts and lean meat. If that sounds like an awful lot of fat, remember this is a percentage of calories (of which fat has many), not of weight.

At the moment the average diet contains more fat and protein than we need and less carbohydrates. Enjoying a

◁ *Pasta is available in a wide variety of shapes and patterns and is an excellent food for boosting your carbohydrate intake. Wholemeal pasta is also particularly high in fibre which helps to speed the passage of waste material through the digestive system.*

△ *Drink plenty of water – 2-3 litres (3.5-5 pints) per day, and more if you are exercising.*

diet rich in starchy carbohydrates has plenty of benefits, not least that they're tasty and filling. Unfortunately, these foods went out of fashion when slimming gurus believed they were fattening. Now we know that starchy foods like rice and potatoes give you energy and should make up the bulk of your diet.

◆ Cut fat to 30 per cent or less. Switch to low-fat dairy products and grill, steam or bake instead of frying.
◆ Increase your fruit and vegetable intake to five portions a day.
◆ Eat only two servings of lean meat or fish a day. A serving equals 55-85g (2-3oz) (enough to cover the palm of your hand).
◆ Eat at least six servings of wholegrain food per day. One serving equals one slice of wholemeal bread, half a bagel, one small roll, half a cup (two heaped tablespoons) of rice, half a cup (two heaped tablespoons) of cooked pasta or three-quarters of a cup (a small bowl) of breakfast cereal.

◆Drink alcohol in moderation. A little wine will help relax you and may even be good for your heart, but too much will make you ill. Limit alcohol intake to 12 units per week (one unit equals a glass of wine, half a pint of beer or one measure of spirits).

◆Increase your calcium intake by eating more low-fat dairy products - aim for three servings per day. A serving equals one cup of skimmed milk (a large 700ml/28fl oz glass),1small pot of low-fat yoghurt (150g/5oz) or cottage cheese (100g/3.5oz) or 40g/1.5oz (a matchbox size) piece of cheese.

◆Eat little and often. Spread your calorie intake throughout the day. Try to eat four small meals, not two large ones.

◆Never skip breakfast.

◆Use unsaturated fats such as olive oil and sunflower oil instead of saturated fats such as butter or lard.

◆Try to choose wholesome , lightly processed foods whenever you can. For example choose oranges over orange drink, wholemeal (wholewheat) over white bread and water rather than fizzy drinks.

◆Lower your salt intake. Less salt can help reduce high blood pressure. Preserved meats such as bacon and pepperoni contain a large quantity of salt and so do many processed foods.

◆Drink plenty of water - 2-3 litres (3.5-5 pints) per day - more if you are exercising.

A healthy diet should include a wide variety of fresh fruit, vegetables, pasta, rice and grains.

Variety

A balanced diet should contain lots of different foods. There is no one magic ingredient – a diet which consists of just apples and carrots is as unhealthy as one of sweets and crisps. The key to health lies in variety: remember every food has its own nutrients. Carrots are rich in beta carotene, which makes vitamin A, and milk is full of calcium.

Moderation

Cut down on junk foods gradually, but try not to make rigid rules for yourself. Remember there's no such thing as a bad or good food. You can eat whatever you want in moderation. Even chocolate, crisps and cakes are OK as long as they are eaten as part of a well balanced diet.

Eating for energy

Everything we eat gives us energy, but some foods are much better than others for boosting our energy supplies. Carbohydrates are the best source of energy and most nutritionists recommend at least 60 per cent of our diet is made up of carbohydrates. So don't be shy about piling your plate with potatoes or rice.

From a nutritional point of view the best types of carbohydrates are the natural sugars found in fruit, vegetables and milk, and complex carbohydrates such as bread, pasta, rice, potatoes, cereals and grains.

◁ *The key to good health lies in a varied diet.*
▽ *Bread is full of healthy carbohydrates.*

Eat less fat

Weight for weight, fat contains more than twice the calories of carbohydrates or protein, so it's easy to eat too much. One gram (.03oz) of fat contains nine calories, so a teaspoon of oil is around 45 calories. What's more, it's easily sucked into our fat cells for storage. Carbohydrates and protein must go through radical changes to be converted to fat, whereas fat is already fat. Since most people want to lose body fat not gain it, it makes sense to cut back.

Too much fat – especially saturated fat – is bad for your heart. The good news is that experts believe it only takes two years following a low-fat diet for most of the benefits to be felt and only five years to see a full reduction in risk. Studies show that lowering our fat intake to 27 per cent of total energy intake (most people eat closer to 40 per cent) and reducing our saturated fat consumption to eight per cent would cause an incredible 50 per cent reduction in deaths from heart disease in people aged 55–64.

△ *A healthy low-fat diet, combined with regular exercise will ensure that you have all the energy you need.*

◆ Cut back on saturated fats. These are solid at room temperature and are mainly found in animal products:
> Butter and cheese
> High-fat meats – sausages, pâté, streaky bacon.
> Cakes
> Chocolate
> Crisps
> Biscuits
> Coconut
> Hydrogenated (hardened) vegetable or fish oils

◆ Unsaturated fats are healthier, but still don't overdo them. They're usually liquid at room temperature and come from vegetable sources:
> Olive oil
> Ground nut oil
> Sunflower oil
> Safflower oil
> Corn oil

ENERGY FOODS
Potatoes
Rice
Bread
Pasta
Bagels
Fruit and vegetables

▽ *Reduce your intake of high-fat foods and eat more 'energy food' such as vegetables, fruit, rice, potatoes, pasta and bread.*

Eat Plants to Live

Every few months yet another new 'superfood' is hailed as a dietary saviour. It seems everything from royal jelly to seaweed has, at some point, been considered the key to health and longevity. Yet the scientific evidence is often shaky and even the experts can't agree whether we should dose up on algae, bee pollen or soya milk. But you don't have to trawl the health food shops or spend a fortune on special pills and potions to enjoy the benefits of true superfoods.

There is now little doubt that more than any other foodstuff, straightforward fruit and vegetables deserve this accolade. Probably one of the only things on which doctors, dieticians and alternative health practitioners all agree is that we should all eat more fresh fruit and vegetables.

Researchers are now confident that a diet rich in fruit and vegetables will reduce our risks of a host of illnesses including heart disease, breast cancer and cancer of the colon. More than 150 studies show that the people who eat most fruit and vegetables are about half as likely to develop cancer as those who eat the least.

Five alive

Almost every health organization recommends that we eat at least 450g (16oz) of fruit and vegetables per day. This excludes potatoes, but includes pulses like beans and chickpeas. Generally the advice is to eat five portions a day. It doesn't matter if they are fresh, frozen or dried. In fact, frozen vegetables often contain more nutrients than fresh.

▷ *Vegetables are packed with nutrients.*

ACE vitamins

Why are fruit and vegetables so good for us? They have many wonderful health properties. They are packed with antioxidant vitamins which include beta carotene (which makes vitamin A in the body) and vitamins C and E – sometimes known as the ACE vitamins. Antioxidants are one the most exciting discoveries in recent years and scientists believe they can help prevent all sorts of degenerative illnesses including cancer, heart disease, arthritis and even ageing of the skin.

◁ The antioxidant vitamins in vegetables can help to prevent a wide variety of degenerative illnesses and protect the body from the harmful effects of pollution and UV light which can damage the body's cells.

◁ Phytochemicals, which occur naturally in plants, are thought to be instrumental in the fight against cancer.

Antioxidants help protect against the harmful effects of smoking, pollution and ultraviolet light which can damage the body's cells.

But antioxidants aren't the only thing in fruit and vegetables to do us good. Now scientists have discovered phytochemicals – a range of obscure but naturally occurring chemicals – which pack an equally powerful disease-fighting punch. Every plant contains hundreds of these chemicals, which fight the damaging effects of sunlight and oxygen. For example, if a bulb of garlic is damaged it produces a chemical called allicin to protect the plant against the invading microbes.

It now seems phytochemicals can help humans too – they're thought to be instrumental in the fight against cancer. Eating a wide range of fruit and vegetables is important because different phytochemicals intervene at different stages of disease.

Fill up on fibre

There are other reasons to eat fruit and vegetables too: fibre, for example. This is the part of plant cells humans can't digest and it comes in two types, soluble and insoluble. Soluble fibre is found in the skin of fruits, vegetables, oats and beans. Insoluble fibre is found in wholemeal bread, brown rice and pasta.

Until a generation ago, fibre was thought useless and was refined out of foods. Hence our diet of white bread, peeled fruits and mashed potatoes. Now we know that the skins of fruit and vegetables as well as the bran in grains are as important to our health as any other nutrient.

Insoluble fibre not only helps move food through our system and prevent constipation, but also protects us from colon cancer, while soluble fibre helps reduce the risk of heart disease. This is because the soluble fibre found in fruit, vegetables and oats affects the absorption of fat and reduces cholesterol levels.

▷ *Start your day with a fibre-rich breakfast of cereal and fruit.*

There's no need to force yourself to sprinkle tasteless wheat bran on your breakfast cereal though: this can actually be harmful, irritating the bowel as well as rushing nutrients through so quickly that they're not properly absorbed.

How to get five servings a day

Unfortunately, a few leaves of lettuce in a hamburger or sandwich don't count as a portion of vegetables.

◆ One portion of vegetables equals two carrots, two heads of broccoli, three tablespoons of peas, two to three tablespoons of cooked spinach, cabbage or runner beans; half a cup of cooked vegetables or one cup of raw vegetables.

◆ One portion of fruit equals one apple, one orange, half a cup of cooked fruit; one cup of raw fruit salad or a six-ounce glass of juice.

◆ Drink a glass of orange juice with your breakfast.

◆ Try chopping some fruit on to your cereals at breakfast.

◆ Take a snack of dried apricots to work as a mid-morning snack – they are a good source of beta carotene.

◆ Steam some greens above your pasta or rice at night.

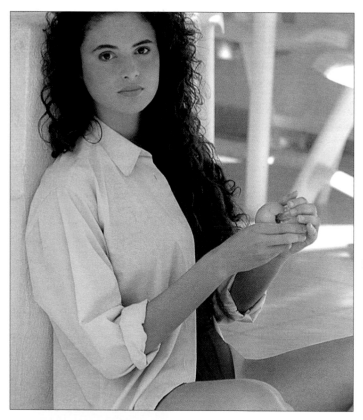

THE TOP 10 HEALTH PROMOTING FOODS

There are hundreds, possibly thousands, of disease-fighting chemicals in plants. Here are some of the best foods you can eat to help keep you healthy.

- Garlic fights cancer.
- Soya beans help prevent cancers of the breast, endometrium and ovary.
- Onions, leeks and chives may slow the development of tumour cells.
- Carrots are a good source of the antioxidant beta carotene.
- Broccoli helps stop carcinogens (cancer-causing agents) damaging our DNA.
- Carrots, celery, parsley and parsnips all help slow down cancerous mutations.
- Oranges are rich in the antioxidant vitamin C and help protect against stomach cancer.
- Vegetable oil is a good source of vitamin E, a potent antioxidant.
- Nuts, seeds and unrefined grains are good sources of dietary fibre which speeds food through the gut, allowing carcinogens less time to interact with the lining.
- Peas are a good source of folic acid, which helps in the formation of red blood cells.

Sensible Slimming

Most women believe they're too fat. There is great pressure on us to be slim in order to look good, but being too thin is just as unhealthy as being overweight. Before you set out to lose weight, ask yourself are you honestly too fat, or are you using your weight as a focus for low self-esteem – feeling bad about yourself in general?

Try to think of food as your friend rather than your enemy and aim to feed your body the best possible fuel, so that you feel well and full of energy. Starving yourself and counting calories are not the answer to low self-esteem, any more than bingeing and filling up on junk foods, and a sensible diet is the best way to lose weight.

Low-calorie diets

Despite hundreds of magazine articles and books warning us of the dangers of very low-calorie diets, many women still choose to crash diet. Practically starving yourself may seem to bring about quick results when you get on the scales, but the results are always short lived.

One reason we tend to put the weight back on is because we have not made any permanent changes to our diet. So try not to think of going on a diet as a short-term solution. Think of food in terms of its overall nutritional qualities. Learn which foods are low in calories and fat and try to make permanent changes which will benefit your overall health, not just your weight.

Some diets recommend special biscuits or milkshakes in place of an ordinary meal. But these 'diet' foods don't have any magic qualities and are often packed with sugar and fat. Some so-called slimming bars contain as much fat as a chocolate bar, and the milkshakes can contain up to six teaspoons of sugar.

If you're absolutely set on using a drink to replace a eal, then whip up a healthy natural version in the liquidizer, using a banana, strawberries and skimmed milk.

How low should you go?

Experts now recommend that we shouldn't cut our calorie intake by more than 500 calories a day. This would mean a reduction of 3,500 calories per week – the equivalent of one pound of body fat. Rather than waste time counting calories, try switching to a low-fat, high-nutrient diet and doing some exercise. Try going for a walk, taking a dance class – or even reading a good book. If you are happy and busy you're less likely to get obsessed by food and overeat in the first place.

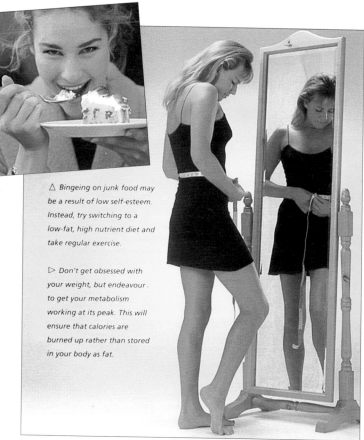

△ Bingeing on junk food may be a result of low self-esteem. Instead, try switching to a low-fat, high nutrient diet and take regular exercise.

▷ Don't get obsessed with your weight, but endeavour to get your metabolism working at its peak. This will ensure that calories are burned up rather than stored in your body as fat.

△ Avoid crash diets – they may help you to lose weight quickly but the results are usually short lived and may encourage weight gain.
◁ The secret to sensible slimming is to eat foods which are nutritious and low in calories, such as pasta, beans and fruit.

Dieting and your metabolism

Low-calorie diets don't work in the long term because they slow down your metabolism – which is the rate at which you burn up calories.

Of course, to lose weight you must eat fewer calories or use up more. But when you eat much less than you need to maintain your weight, your body goes into famine-mode and reacts by slowing the metabolism, so you burn fewer calories a day – the opposite of what you want. When you go back to eating normally, the body holds on to extra calories to rebuild the fat stores.

Millions of women have fallen prey to yo-yo dieting – shedding weight on a low-calorie diet, piling it back on with more besides afterwards, then having to cut calories even further to lose any weight the next time. But if you're one of them, don't let worries about your metabolism get you down. While failed diets may have slowed your metabolism temporarily, they're unlikely to have done any permanent damage.

Being overweight is more likely to be down to what you are eating than to a slow metabolism. If you are heavily overweight, don't lose heart: just change to healthy eating patterns and take some more exercise.

Yo-yo dieting and your heart

The true danger of yo-yo dieting probably lies in where the fat is redeposited. When the weight is put back on after a bout of dieting it is more likely to be deposited on the abdominal region. So a woman may lose weight from her thighs and put it back on around her waist.

This may not sound so bad if you hate your bottom-heavy shape. But medical evidence suggests that fat stored on your stomach is worse for your heart than fat stored on your hips or thighs. This may be one reason men, who tend to be apple-shaped, are more likely to suffer from heart disease than women, who are generally pear-shaped.

Making permanent changes

Often diets fail because we expect too much, too soon. Small changes you can make and stick to will have more lasting effects than drastic measures which last only a couple of weeks.

How much fat do we need?

Cutting the fat in your diet will help you lose weight. It will also reduce your risk of cancer. Everyone should try to cut fat to 30 per cent of their daily calories. For a woman on 2,000 calories a day, that means 70g (2.5oz) of fat. If you are trying to lose weight, it's best to cut your fat intake further, say to 20 or 25 per cent (around 50g (1.75oz) fat per day).

CUTTING DOWN ON FAT

◆ Use semi-skimmed milk on your cereals. Semi-skimmed milk has all the nutrients of whole milk but only 10g (0.35oz) of fat per pint, compared to 23g (0.8oz) of fat in whole milk. Make cheese sauces and custards with skimmed milk – you won't notice the difference.
◆ Skip mayonnaise-saturated sandwich fillings. A heaped tablespoon of mayonnaise contains 22g (.75oz) of fat.
◆ Always make sure butter is soft before you spread it – you'll use less.
◆ Eat baked potatoes instead of french fries.
◆ Use low-fat fromage frais and chives on baked potatoes, instead of butter or sour cream.
◆ Use lean back bacon instead of streaky and trim off the fat.
◆ Remove the skin from turkey and chicken before you eat it. Roast chicken with its skin contains a lot more fat (14 per cent) than roast topside of beef (4.4 per cent).
◆ Order your pizza topped with grilled vegetables instead of beef and pastrami. Ask them to hold the cheese.
◆ Buy lean cuts of meat and skip high-fat sausages, bacon and mince.
◆ Make omelettes with egg whites instead of whole eggs.

◁ Cutting the fat in your diet will help you to lose weight and will also reduce your risk of cancer. You should try to cut your intake of fat to 30 per cent of your daily calories generally, and reduce that further to 20 per cent if you are trying to lose weight.
▷ Monounsaturated fats, such as those found in avocados, are useful in the fight against high levels of cholesterol.

Most experts agree that we shouldn't cut our fat intake more drastically, as this can bring its own health problems. Essential fatty acids are needed to build our cell membranes and for other vital bodily functions. Don't forget we need some body fat for brain tissue, nerve sheaths and bone marrow. We also need fat to protect our vital organs such as the heart, liver and kidneys. Women need extra fat stored on the breasts and hips for normal hormone production and fertility.

▷ *Be careful not to cut fat too drastically – some fat is necessary for the development of cell structures, brain tissue and bone marrow, and women need to store extra reserves on breasts and hips for hormone production.*

Healthy Meal Planning

Try to eat roughly similar numbers of calories at each meal. Remember, food eaten earlier in the day fires the metabolism and gives us energy, whereas food eaten late at night tends to be laid down and stored as fat. So breakfast like a king, lunch like a prince and dine like a pauper!

Some people complain that eating breakfast makes them feel hungrier and eat more later on. But studies have shown the opposite is true: breakfast-eaters consume fewer calories and less fat throughout the rest of the day. If you are hungry again immediately after breakfast, it's probably a sign that you still haven't eaten enough.

Start the day with plenty of energy-rich food and choose a carbohydrate-rich, low-fat breakfast to get through a busy morning. It's worth getting up a little earlier and giving yourself time to wake up with a good breakfast, instead of waiting for hunger to strike mid-morning when the only handy options seem to be sugary doughnuts or chocolate. As the suggestions opposite show, healthy eating tastes good too.

If you do feel hungry between meals, snack on fresh fruit, bagels, pretzels or dried fruit and a few raw nuts. But remember dried fruit and nuts are high energy foods, so don't overdo them if you are trying to lose weight.

▷ *When you are planning healthy meals it is essential to include plenty of fresh vegetables. Aim for at least five portions of different vegetables and frûit per day and remember that vitamins A, C and the B group may be destroyed when your food is cooked.*

BREAKFAST

◆ Porridge oats with semi-skimmed milk, banana and raisins – or ring the changes with your favourite dried fruit.

◆ Two slices of wholemeal toast with honey and an orange.

◆ One cup – 100g (4oz) of mixed, chopped fruit with a carton of low-fat yoghurt; one slice of wholemeal toast and honey.

◆ Two slices of wholemeal toast and low-fat cottage cheese with a glass of orange juice.

◆ A large bowl of bran flakes, with chopped banana and semi-skimmed milk.

LUNCH

◆ Whole-meal pitta bread stuffed with hummus or chickpeas, cottage cheese and salad. Followed by low-fat yoghurt.

◆ Wholewheat sandwich with turkey and salad. Glass of skimmed milk.

◆ Baked potato with baked beans and low-fat grated cheese; bowl of salad and an apple.

◆ Rice salad made with 85g (3oz) rice, mushrooms, peppers, tomatoes, pineapple, one egg and two kiwi fruit for dessert.

◆ A large salad of all your favourite leaves – some supermarkets now sell ready washed mixed packs – with cherry tomatoes. Lemon juice makes a no-fat dressing, or mix a small amount of oil with malt or wine vinegar, a pinch of salt and, if you like, some mustard. Serve with wholemeal bread and tuna fish in brine (not oil).

DINNER

◆ Homemade vegetable and bean soup and a wholegrain roll; half a mango for dessert.

◆ 85g (3oz) spaghetti and home-made tomato sauce sprinkled with parmesan cheese; baked apple and yoghurt.

◆ Grilled chicken, 85g (3oz) brown rice, broccoli, carrots; one low-fat yoghurt and a banana.

◆ 140g (5oz) white fish, medium jacket potato, portion of beans and carrots; baked banana and fromage frais.

◆ Kebabs with lean meat, peppers, tomatoes; 85g (3oz) rice and broccoli; 110g (4oz) fruit salad.

Eating to Prevent Osteoporosis

One elderly woman in three suffers from the brittle-bone disease osteoporosis, which is a major cause of back pain and fractures. Frighteningly, this crippling illness is now becoming less of a rarity among young women. Everyone needs calcium to build strong bones, but most of us aren't getting enough. According to one survey, 20 per cent of young girls get much less than they need and the pattern continues as they grow older.

△ *Limit the amount of coffee you drink as it depletes the body's supply of calcium, which is needed to keep bones strong and healthy.*

Doctors are now blaming slimming diets for the upsurge of osteoporosis among women in their twenties and thirties, long before it should be a problem. (It's also tied in with the female hormone oestrogen, which is why it's so common after the menopause.)

Although adults stop growing at the age of 20, their bones don't reach peak density until 30–35. After the age of 35 bones start to thin, but a calcium-rich diet, together with regular weight-bearing exercise, can help to prevent them from becoming weak or brittle.

All women should eat three or four servings of calcium-rich food every day – 85-140g (3-5oz) to help build strong bones and prevent osteoporosis. Menopausal and pregnant women need more: at least four servings per day. And if you're tempted to give up dairy products to try to keep your weight down, bear in mind that skimmed milk has all the calcium with hardly any fat content.

A lack of the mineral magnesium seems to add to the problem, by preventing the body from absorbing the calcium properly. It's found in meat, seafoods, green vegetables and, again, dairy products. Don't overdo the meat, though, as too much protein also contributes to osteoporosis by making the body excrete calcium.

◁ *Skimmed milk is one of the richest sources of calcium, with hardly any fat content.*

△ ◁ ▽ *Muesli, low-fat yoghurt and sunflower oil all help to increase your calcium levels.*

♦ Try to include a calcium-rich food with every meal.

♦ The best sources of calcium are low-fat milk, yoghurt and low-fat cheese.

♦ One serving of calcium-rich food equals 40g (1.5oz) of cheese, one 200ml (8floz) glass of milk or a 200ml (8floz) serving of yoghurt.

♦ Non-dairy sources of calcium include broccoli, canned sardines and salmon (with bones), tofu, pulses, muesli with nuts, and white bread.

♦ Limit consumption of salt, coffee, sugar and alcohol, as these deplete calcium supplies.

♦ Remember that there's caffeine in chocolate and cola drinks as well as in coffee – even tea contains a little caffeine.

♦ Cut down on smoking for the same reason. Along with all the other havoc smoking wreaks on your body, it reduces production of oestrogen,.

♦ Increase your consumption of essential fatty acids (EFAs) found in oily fish, sunflower and safflower oil. EFAs increase calcium absorption.

Eating for Pregnancy

Everyone knows that what you eat, drink or smoke while pregnant can affect your baby. Now experts believe that what you eat even before you get pregnant can have an influence too. Ideally your body should be in great shape before you get pregnant. So if you're planning a baby, start filling up on healthy nutrient-rich foods now, cut right back on alcohol and stop smoking.

One of the main questions that concerns pregnant women is 'how much should I eat?' Many women still believe they should be eating for two, but that's a myth. Calorie requirements don't really increase during pregnancy, except in the last three months when you may need around an extra 200 calories per day.

Although you don't really need to eat much more, you shouldn't diet either. You should make sure all the food you eat is packed with goodness, as you need extra nutrients at this time. Although you should be able to get all your nutrients from your diet, it may be a good idea to take a multivitamin supplement as an extra precaution.

▷ *When you are pregnant, you should ensure that you eat food that is packed with goodness as it is important to get extra nutrients at this time.*

Vitamins and minerals

Pregnant women should make sure they are getting enough folic acid because this nutrient has been shown to reduce the chance of having a baby with a neural tube defect such as spina bifida. You can increase your intake by eating lots of fruit and vegetables such as broccoli, baked potatoes, spinach and bananas. Some cereals are also fortified with folic acid. However, doctors still advise any woman planning a pregnancy to take a

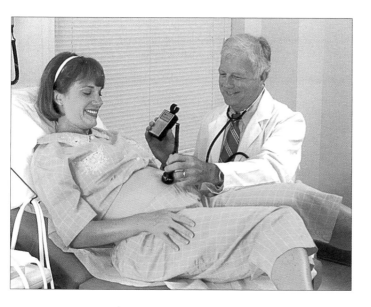

Alcohol

It's safest to cut out alcohol altogether during pregnancy - especially during the first three months. Any alcohol can cross over the placenta and affect the baby; heavy drinking will almost certainly be harmful.

Also avoid mould-ripened cheeses such as Camembert or Brie and blue-veined cheese such as Stilton which may be contaminated with listeria bacteria. Though quite rare, this can be harmful to the unborn child.

Pregnant women should avoid vitamin A supplements and liver (which contains high quantities of this vitamin), since high levels have been linked to birth defects. Vitamin A or beta carotene found in other food such as milk, cheese, eggs and carrots is perfectly safe.

supplement of folic acid each day, from before conception until the twelfth week of pregnancy.

Pregnant women need extra calcium for building the baby's bones. So make

△ *Ensure that you have regular medical check-ups throughout your pregnancy.*
▷ *Cut out alcohol, and stop smoking.*

△ *The recommended weight gain for the entire pregnancy is 8.8-14.2kg (20-32lb).*

sure you eat plenty of calcium-rich food like yoghurt, low-fat milk and cheese. If you don't get enough during pregnancy it will affect the long-term health of your own bones and you will be more likely to suffer from osteoporosis.

Extra iron is needed to manufacture red blood cells. Women who fall short on this nutrient during pregnancy are more likely to develop anaemia after the birth. So make sure you eat iron-rich foods such as beef, chicken, sardines, Weetabix, baked beans, wholemeal bread, spinach and broccoli. It may be advisable to take an iron supplement - but check with your doctor first as these tend to cause constipation.

Zinc is needed for healthy cell division and is important for the baby's growth. If you have been advised to take an iron supplement you may need zinc too, as extra iron reduces zinc absorption.

Superfood Supplements

What are minerals and vitamins? They are needed in tiny amounts for healthy growth and maintenance of all the body's cells. Serious deficiencies can lead to illnesses such as rickets (vitamin D) or scurvy (vitamin C), while minor deficiencies can cause lack of energy and poor skin. The shelves of health food stores are loaded with bottles of vitamin pills and food supplements, but doctors still aren't convinced we need to take them. Generally the advice is to make sure you are getting all the nutrients you need from the food you eat.

△ *Studies have shown that garlic helps to prevent blood clots, is good for your heart and can lower cholesterol.*

Vitamins and minerals that come in pills don't have all the other benefits of nutrient-rich foods, like dietary fibre which protects against bowel cancer, or phytochemicals such as polyphenols and flavenoids which also help fight disease.

However, some nutritionists believe it may be difficult for women to get all the nutrients they need from their diet alone. One thing everyone agrees on is that to get all you need you must follow all the guidelines for a healthy diet. The trouble is, lots of us don't, so there's probably no harm in taking a multivitamin.

If you decide to take supplements it would be best to see a nutritionist first, to carefully analyze your diet and decide which nutrients you need. Follow the instructions on the bottle and don't be tempted to take more than recommended.

Taking more than you need won't do you any good and is a waste of money. Some vitamins can even be harmful when taken in excess. For example high doses of vitamin A accumulate in the liver and can be poisonous.

Superfood supplements

'Superfood' supplements such as garlic, fish oil, evening primrose oil and algae capsules may make a useful contribution to your health. Opposite are some the best, but don't forget it should be possible to get the same benefits by eating a varied and healthy diet.

▽ *Raw garlic is one of the most potent natural tonics and helps to fight infections.*

SUPERFOODS

◆ Garlic is a powerful tonic when it comes to fighting infections and is also good for colds. Studies show garlic helps prevent blood clots, is good for your heart and can lower cholesterol. It even helps protect against stomach cancer. Raw garlic is more potent than cooked.

◆ Fish oils Omega-3 polyunsaturated fatty acids (PUFAs) protect against heart disease, blood clotting and high blood pressure. They also help check rheumatoid arthritis and the skin disorder psoriasis. They can be found in salmon, mackerel and sardines.

◆ Evening primrose oil is a rich source of gamma-linolenic acid (GLA), which helps keeps the body healthy. It can improve the condition of your skin and nails as well as easing premenstrual syndrome (PMS) and high blood pressure. Recommended for eczema and breast soreness. Top up your GLA levels with fresh vegetables, vegetable oils, wheat, maize and soya beans.

◆ Ginkgo – this prehistoric plant can increase alertness and slow the onset of senility.

◆ Algae such as chlorella and spirulina have been hailed as the new 'wonderfoods'. They are rich in nutrients – particularly protein, iron, beta carotene, vitamin B12 (especially needed by vegans, who eat no meat, dairy produce or eggs) and chlorophyll, which is said to help the body clear out harmful toxins. Many nutritionists, though, claim you can get all these benefits from a diet rich in fruit and vegetables.

▷ 'Superfood' supplements are available in a wide variety of tablets and capsules.

Food Allergies

A real food allergy is a serious condition with severe symptoms which appear immediately after the offending food is eaten. Reactions may include vomiting, diarrhoea, swelling and rashes. In the worst scenario the victim can go into anaphylactic shock: they start to wheeze, their blood pressure falls sharply and they may even pass out. The most common causes of anaphylaxis are nuts and shellfish.

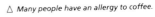

△ *Many people have an allergy to coffee.*

A food allergy can develop out of the blue, after a lifetime of eating a food without any problems. Fortunately these severe allergies are rare. More often people suffer from food intolerance or sensitivity, but these are harder to recognize and many doctors don't even accept they exist.

Symptoms thought to be caused by food sensitivity include headaches, stomach pains and bloating, migraine, aching joints and muscles, hay fever and irritability. Some practitioners even blame weight gain on food sensitivity, although most doctors are very sceptical about this.

The problem lies in proving which food is to blame, since symptoms are not immediate and can emerge after several days rather than immediately after eating the problem food. The usual way to find the culprit is through an exclusion diet on which you eat a small number of harmless foods, then gradually reintroduce other foods until you start having symptoms again, which identifies the offenders. The foods which are most often blamed for intolerances are wheat and dairy produce.

However, beware of restricting your diet unnecessarily, as leaving out whole food groups can make your diet unbalanced and cause you to miss out on vital nutrients. Women in particular should be wary of eliminating dairy products without taking steps to replace the bone-strengthening calcium.

The best way to avoid a food intolerance is to eat and drink a wide range of foods in moderation. Overloading on a particular food may prevent your body producing enough enzymes to digest it properly. Researchers have found that even people who are intolerant to milk can drink a small amount – about a glass a day – without any symptoms.

If you suspect an allergy or food intolerance, seek advice from your doctor or ask to be referred to a specialist allergy clinic.

▽ *Shellfish are a common cause of allergic reactions, some of which can be most unpleasant.*

Is it an allergy or faddy eating?

Food intolerances seem to be very fashionable at the moment and dieticians are concerned that many women use the excuse of a so-called allergy as a way to restrict their diet for weight-loss purposes. If avoiding a food makes you feel better all well and good, but don't fall into the trap of over-restricting your diet and missing out on the vital nutrients you need.

What can I do about an allergy?

A food allergy or intolerance may disappear as mysteriously as it appeared, but in the meantime you should avoid the troublesome food. If you are allergic to cow's milk try switching to goat's milk and cheese; or try soya products available from most health food stores.

If you are allergic to wheat, swap to rye bread and make sure you get enough starch by eating more rice, barley and other grains.

Don't forget wheat and milk powder are found in all sorts of processed food, so you will need to check the labels carefully.

△ Even if you are allergic to milk you may still be able to drink a small amount without any ill effect. You can also switch to goat's milk or soya milk if allergic symptoms persist.

△ Some people find that they have an intolerance to strawberries.

▷ Food allergies can cause headaches, nausea, or even anaphylactic shock in the case of a reaction to nuts.

Coping with Stress

Worries about money, work, family and relationships are major sources of stress for women. Sometimes we can do something about our situation and sometimes we can't. In any event, coping strategies are our best line of defence.

Unfortunately when we are under pressure, many of us do things that make us feel worse, not better. We binge on comfort foods, go on spending sprees, lie awake at night, and shout at our friends and family! So what can we do instead?

Talk it over

Don't keep all your worries to yourself. Try discussing your problems with an objective friend or member of your family. People who bottle up their problems suffer from stress more than those who get them out in the open.

Experts believe that bottled up tensions can make us ill by increasing our blood pressure and cholesterol levels.

Take a deep breath

If your heart's racing and you can feel yourself starting to panic, try taking a deep breath, or six. Six deep breaths should be enough to reduce your blood pressure and calm you down.

Learn to breathe deeply and fully as this relaxes the body, whereas quick panicky breaths make you feel worse.

Place your hand on your chest and as you breathe in slowly feel your lungs expand. As you breath out, your chest and stomach will deflate. Continue this until you start to feel calmer.

Go for a walk

When you are feeling upset or stressed, exercise can act as a powerful anti-depressant. Going for a walk or run gets rid of the adrenalin our bodies pump out when we're feeling stressed and helps us let off steam. After aerobic exercise, stress hormones are reduced and the body experiences a natural relaxation response.

Take a hot bath

When you're ready to scream, escape to the bathroom and take a long, hot bath. Sometimes all you need is a little time and space for yourself. So hang a 'do not disturb' sign on the bathroom door and sink into a bath with a few drops of relaxing lavender aromatherapy oil. Aromatherapy oils are a wonderful way to calm a constant stream of brain-chatter or 'busymind'.

Cut down on caffeine

You might think a few strong cups of coffee can get you through the day, but your addiction could be making you more stressed out, especially if you are sensitive to caffeine.

Even tea contains some caffeine, so if you drink too much of either at night you'll feel less refreshed in the morning. They take six hours to work their way through your system and as little as two cups of coffee a day could affect your sleep patterns. Caffeine reduces the time we spend dreaming – which we need, as dream sleep is the brain's way of unwinding.

◁ *Bottled up stress can make us ill by raising blood pressure and cholesterol levels.*
▷ *Relax in a hot bath, laced with a few drops of lavender aromatherapy oil.*

Work out your priorities

When there's too much to do and not enough time, make a 'to do' list and set some priorities. Ask yourself what things are most important and urgent – do these first. Don't let yourself be distracted by all the small jobs. Set yourself one or two major tasks a day and update your list on a regular basis.

Try not to leave things until the last minute and if you can't get a task completed by the deadline, then let the relevant people know rather than avoiding them. Don't let guilt add to your stress levels.

△ *Place one hand on your chest and breathe in slowly, feeling your lungs expand.*

△ *Breathe out, noticing your chest and stomach deflate. Continue until you feel calm.*

△ *Make time in your day to relax with some soothing music, or read a good book.*

Exercise for Body and Mind

Our bodies were designed for movement, and without exercise they start to degenerate. Unfortunately these days most of us lead sedentary lives. We drive to the supermarket, we sit at a desk and collapse onto the sofa to watch television. It's no wonder obesity is becoming a Western epidemic.

Everyone should exercise, whatever their age, and no matter how busy they are. If you do nothing else for your health, at the very least, make the effort to become more active.

Imagine that someone told you there was a wonderful new slimming treatment than not only helped keep weight off but also reduced your risk of heart disease, strokes, cancer and osteoporosis. Not only that, but it didn't cost anything. You'd certainly consider trying it, wouldn't you?

Despite all these benefits, many women still don't take any exercise at all. But exercise not only has lots of long-term health benefits   it can help you look and feel great too.

Exercise helps you relax by getting rid of excess adrenalin and can help you sleep well at night. Some women even find exercise relieves premenstrual syndrome and period pains. Other studies have found exercise is as effective as drugs in tackling depression.

What kind of exercise?

You don't have to go to a health club or use any special equipment to exercise,

although some women find it easier to exercise in this kind of environment. It's always helpful to have expert instructors on hand to help you design a good fitness programme.

Any routine should include three different elements: exercise for strength, aerobic training for cardiovascular fitness and flexibility work.

▷ *Exercise reduces the risk of heart disease and helps to keep weight off. Make it a fun part of your leisure activities.*

Flexibility

Stretching becomes increasingly important as we get older and start to stiffen up. But with regular flexibility exercises, there's no need to lose mobility as we age. Stretching, yoga, swimming and dance classes are all excellent ways of staying flexible.

◁ *Muscles can be toned and strengthened by regular weight training sessions at your local gym.*

▽ *Aerobic exercise is essential for ensuring cardiovascular fitness, so include running, cycling, swimming or simple dance routines in your training programme. You can work out at home, or join an aerobics class.*

Strength

Muscle strength can be improved by weight training in a gym, or by doing exercises such as press-ups which use your own body weight to challenge your muscles. Many women shy away from weight training, fearing they'll end up musclebound and unfeminine. In fact, it's unbelievably difficult for women to build that kind of shape — our hormones work against creating muscles like that.

Cardiovascular fitness

Running, brisk walking, aerobics classes, swimming, skating, cycling and stair climbing are all excellent types of aerobic exercise. Done regularly they will help you burn excess body fat and strengthen your heart and lungs.

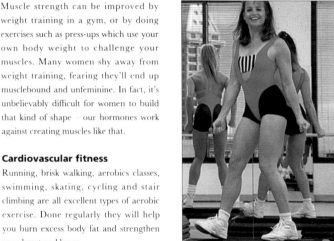

◁ *Stretching exercises or simple yoga positions will help to keep your body flexible. This is particularly important as you get older and start to stiffen.*

Weight Training

Women often stay away from the gym because they think of weight training as a man's exercise. We worry that lifting weights may make us bigger rather than slimmer. So we opt instead for aerobics or other sports. But women won't build bulky muscles because they don't normally have the right hormones. If you want to streamline your shape, weight training is one of the best things you can do.

A major factor in how good we look is our muscle-to-fat ratio. Reshaping your body means reducing the fat through diet and exercise, while developing muscle tone by weight training.

It's good for burning off calories, too. You use up around 400 calories an hour when you're training with weights. What's more, it can give your metabolism a long-term boost: lean muscle tissue burns more calories than fat, so more muscle mass means a higher metabolism – not only in the gym but all day too, which is good news if you are trying to lose weight. It's no wonder studies have shown that weight training is particularly good for improving self-confidence and body image.

As you get older, weight training will help stop middle-age spread. As people age they tend to lose muscle tissue – usually at the rate of 2.25-2.75kg (5-6lb) each decade. This means that your metabolism slows down and you gain unwanted body fat. Training with weights can counteract these changes.

There are lots of health bonuses too for all ages; you don't have to be young to see the benefits. Weight-bearing exercise can help build strong bones and help prevent osteoporosis. One study of post-menopausal women found that just two 45-minute sessions a week were sufficient to maintain bone density.

New research has even found weight training can aid digestion and reduce the risk of colon cancer. Food travels twice as fast through the bodies of people who pump iron, reducing the chances of cancer-causing substances being absorbed.

Weight training is a good choice if you want to prevent back problems. Back pain is often due to weak muscles, and one study found 80 per cent of people's back pain improved when they strengthened their muscles in this area.

It helps with sports too, by making you more resistant to injuries.

◁ **KICKBACKS**

Using a bench or strong chair for balance, lean forward and rest your left hand on the bench, holding a dumbbell in your right hand. Keep your back straight and lift your upper arm until it is parallel with the floor.

Lift the dumbbell back until your entire arm is straight and parallel to the floor. hold for a few seconds, then slowly lower your arm as you breathe in.

▷ **FRONT SHOULDER LIFTS**

Stand with feet apart and back straight. Hold a dumbbell in each hand with palms facing towards the front of your body. Breathe out as you raise your right arm in front of you until the weight is at shoulder height and hold. Breathe in as you slowly lower your arm. Repeat 10 times with each arm.

◁ BENT OVER ROWING

Use a strong chair, bench or other sturdy object for balance. Lean on the chair with your right hand and hold a dumbbell in your left hand, ensuring that your arm is extended straight down towards the floor.

Keep your shoulders square to the floor and your arm close to your body at all times and pull the dumbbell straight up towards your chest as you breathe out. Slowly lower the dumbbell to the starting position as you breathe in. Repeat the exercise 10 times using each arm.

◁ FRENCH SQUATS

Stand with your feet a little more than shoulder width apart. Take a disc weight and hold it with both hands crossed in front of your chest. Slowly breathe in and lower your body until your thighs are parallel to the floor. Breathe out as you tighten your buttocks and return to the standing position. Repeat the exercise 10 times.

This exercise may also be performed without using weights, without significantly reducing the benefit to your muscles.

TRAINING TIPS

◆ Aim for two to four weight training sessions per week.

◆ Always perform exercises with 'good form', meaning that every exercise should be done in a slow, controlled way.

◆ Allow at least a day for your muscles to recover between weight training sessions.

◆ Follow a programme devised by a qualified instructor.

◆ If you have high blood pressure, see your doctor before you start weight training.

Aerobic Exercise

Besides burning calories and reducing body fat, aerobic exercise will help relieve stress, strengthen your heart and lower your blood pressure. Women who exercise regularly also reduce their risk of life-threatening illnesses including breast cancer, heart disease and diabetes.

△ *Learn how to take your own pulse and work out your maximum heart rate.*

If you're still not motivated, consider this: people who exercise regularly have more confidence, higher energy levels and, some even say, better orgasms.

Any exercise which pushes your heart rate up and makes you breathe harder is aerobic. Swimming, running, fast walking, trampolining, cycling: what you choose is up to you. It's a good idea to vary your workouts, as different exercises train different muscles and the more variety your fitness programme includes, the less your chance of boredom or injury.

The most important thing is to do something regularly. Ideally you should aim to get out of breath at least once a day and aim for one continuous 20-minute session at least three times per week. If you can't manage 20 minutes, aim for several 10-minute exercise sessions every day.

If formal exercise is out of the question, try to make your life more active: walk to the shops instead of taking the car and use the stairs instead of the lift – every little counts.

◆ Start off gently. Gradually increase the time and intensity of your workouts.
◆ To lose weight, increase the length and intensity of your workouts. To lose body fat you need to burn more calories.

Exercise Intensity

To improve your fitness you must push yourself so that your heart rate increases and you feel slightly out of breath, but not so out of breath that you can't talk. Your heart is like any other muscle and must be challenged if it is to increase in strength.

Fitness experts say we should work at a level between 60 and 85 per cent of our maximum heart rate. Your maximum heart rate – the theoretical fastest pulse for your age – is 220 minus your age. So if you are 30 your maximum heart rate is 190, and you should be aiming for 114–161 beats per minute when you're exercising. In this 'training zone' we burn most body fat and make most fitness gains.

Taking Your Pulse

Learning to take your pulse properly will take a bit of practice. You must take an accurate reading, though, or you could end up working at an unsuitable level.

Find the radial artery on the thumb side of your wrist and count the beats for 15 seconds, then multiply by four for the number of beats per minute. Try taking your

▷ *Aerobic exercise pushes up your heart rate and makes you breathe harder.*

△ *A rebounder will allow you to exercise aerobically, without straining your knees.*

▷ *You will need to replace fluid lost as sweat when you exercise, so take water breaks every 15-20 minutes during your training sessions.*

pulse every five minutes while you exercise and compare it with the figure for your theoretical fastest pulse. Beginners should aim for 60 to 70 per cent of their maximum heart rate. Advanced exercisers can push themselves harder.

If you find taking your pulse too difficult, you may like to invest in an electronic pulse monitor which takes your pulse for you. Or the easiest way is to watch out for signs of discomfort and simply slow down. Remember exercise isn't supposed to hurt.

REHYDRATION
Remember to take regular water breaks. When you sweat you need to replace lost fluid. Fitness experts recommend 2 cups of fluid 2 hours before exercise and one full cup every 15 – 20 minutes during exercise.

Walk Yourself Fit

Walking is an excellent way to get fit, especially if you are just starting out. Regular walking can help maintain a healthy weight and burn body fat. It puts little stress on your knees or body, so it's suitable for anyone: young or old, fit or unfit.

Like any exercise the benefits will depend on how much you do and how hard you push yourself. A gentle stroll on a Sunday afternoon won't instantly boost your fitness levels, but you don't have to be an Olympic power walker to see the benefits either.

One recent study found that walking 3km (2 miles) a day at any pace reduces your risk of coronary heart disease. Moderate walking will also lower the bad cholesterol in your blood and help build strong bones, protecting women against osteoporosis. It's also a great way of letting off steam and boosting your energy levels. The rhythmic, repetitive movement can be calming and soothing and may even stimulate creative thinking.

Many women find jogging or running uncomfortable, especially if they are unfit; it's also common for women to suffer from knee problems, so running is painful. Walking is a wonderful alternative. All you need is a pair of good walking shoes and you are ready to go.

Walking at a gentle pace is certainly good for you, but if you really want to see the fitness benefits, power walking is best.

▷ *Walking is good at any speed and even a gentle stroll will help you to relax. Regular walking of 3km (2 miles) per day will reduce your chances of coronary heart disease.*

Try picking up your pace and pumping your arms. You should be walking quite fast – as if you are late for an appointment. At this pace, you will improve your cardiovascular fitness and give your body a good all-over workout. Walking will tone your legs, buttocks, abdominals and upper body.

Power walking at a fast pace burns even more calories than slow jogging, because brisk walking requires pure effort, whereas jogging can rely on momentum.

△ *Moderate walking will help to reduce cholesterol levels and build strong bones.*

Technique
Posture Check: Relax your shoulders. Keep your neck long and chin parallel to the ground – try focusing on a point 4.5m (15ft) in front. Lift and open your chest. Don't arch your back. Keep your stomach tight and hips square.

Stepping Action.
◆ Put your foot down from heel to toe.
◆ Lengthen your stride as you speed up.
◆ Keep your arms bent at 90 degrees and swing them in time with your step.

◁ *Start by walking on flat ground until you are ready to progress to more strenuous terrain. As you get fitter, increase your walking pace and pump your arms to increase your cardiovascular fitness and tone your upper body as well as your legs.*

THE WALKING WORKOUT
◆ Aim for at least three 30-minute sessions per week.
◆ If you can't spare half an hour do 10 minutes instead – every little counts.
◆ Warm up slowly: gently increase your speed.
◆ If you are unfit, start off at a gentle pace. Three kilometres per hour (2mph) may be enough to increase your heart rate so you are in your training zone. As you get fitter, pick up the pace to 6-8km/h (4-5mph).
◆ You should be slightly breathless, but not gasping.
◆ Start by walking on flat terrain. As you get fitter you can try gentle hills for a more challenging workout.
◆ Don't forget to stretch after your workout. Stretch all your major muscle groups – calves are especially important, otherwise they will tighten up and make your shins sore.

Run for Your Life

Running is an excellent way of lifting your mood and burning off anxiety and stress. It doesn't suit everyone and it's certainly a tough way to start your fitness routine, so don't feel disheartened if you can only manage five minutes at first.

As with any aerobic exercise, running will help you burn off extra body fat and reduce your risk of heart disease. You'll burn between 200 and 400 calories on a 30-minute run, depending on your body weight and speed.

The faster or heavier you are, the more you will burn. But take care: if you are very overweight it's probably best to start with a low-impact activity like swimming or walking. Running is a high-impact activity and can stress the joints, particularly the knees.

A good pair of proper running shoes is essential to cushion and support your foot and will reduce your risk of injury. Running on grass or treadmill will also reduce the impact on your joints.

Technique
◆ Relax your shoulders and upper body.
◆ Don't clench your fists.
◆ Keep your arms bent at 90 degrees.

Posture Check
See the Walking section.

The Running Workout
◆ Always start with a warm-up: five to 10 minutes fast walking or marching on the spot.
◆ Next stretch all your major muscle groups, especially your legs: calves, hamstrings and quads. You must stretch again after your run.
◆ Don't do too much too soon – you're far more likely to get an injury. Never increase your running distance or time by more than 10 per cent a week.
◆ Don't stop suddenly as the blood will pool in your legs and make you feel dizzy. Instead slow down gradually, to a brisk walk, then a stroll.
◆ Beginners should start at a gentle pace and gradually build up their jogging time to 20 minutes three times a week.
◆ As you get fitter you can build up your time and vary the pace. Try boosting your fitness with hill running or interval training.

▽ *Always start with a warm up – march on the spot for 5-10 minutes, then stretch all of your major muscle groups. Remember to stretch them again after your run.*

Interval Training

Interval training is a great way to vary your workout and boost your fitness levels. It basically means varying the pace and is a technique used by athletes to push themselves to the next fitness level. The technique can be used for any form of aerobic exercise – running, swimming, cycling or walking – and is a great way to make exercise more fun.

Warm up and stretch as usual. Next run at a gentle pace for two minutes, then run very fast for 30 seconds. Repeat this sequence six times. As you get fitter you can boost the pace for two minutes and then slow it down for one.

△ You should stop for water breaks at regular intervals to avoid dehydration.
◁ As your performance improves, you can increase your time and vary your pace, or include interval training or hill running.

△ Relax your shoulders, keep your chin parallel to the ground and your hips square.

Pedal Power

Cycling can improve your cardiovascular fitness, burn body fat and strengthen and tone the muscles in your legs and buttocks. It's also a low-impact activity and is easier on the joints than running.

Whether you choose to cycle on the road or on a stationary bike in a health club, both have their benefits. Road cycling appeals to people who find gyms boring and is a great form of transport. But if you live in a city with lots of traffic you may prefer the safety of a stationary bike at home or in the gym.

Technique

Make sure your saddle is at the correct height. When you are standing next to your bike the saddle should be level with the top of your hip. When you are cycling make sure your legs are almost fully extended with a slight bend in the knee at the bottom point of the revolution. A seat which is too low will make it harder to cycle and will be uncomfortable.

Safety

◆ Always wear a helmet when cycling on roads or when mountain biking.
◆ Use lights and reflective clothing at night.

Buying a Home Exercise Bike

Before you buy an exercise bike ask yourself if you will really use it. Any piece of equipment that just ends up cluttering your garage is a waste of money. If you are a complete beginner or lack willpower and motivation, you may be better off spending your money on gym membership or 10 sessions with a personal trainer.

▽ *Cycling is an enjoyable way to improve your general fitness and tone leg muscles.*

THE WORKOUT

◆ Start off by pedalling at a low resistance in an easy gear for five minutes.

◆ Beginners should aim for three 10-minutes sessions a week and build up gradually to 20 minutes three times a week.

◆ For a more advanced workout introduce interval training. This means playing with the gears if you are cycling on the road or the resistance level on a stationary bike.

• Cycle hard against a strong resistance for one minutes, then reduce the resistance for 30 seconds.

• Repeat five to 10 times.

• If you are training on a stationary bike, make sure you cycle at 80 rpm (revolutions per minute).

◆ Aim to cycle continuously. If you keep stopping and starting at road junctions and traffic lights you'll still burn calories, but you won't get all the fitness benefits of a continuous 20-minute workout.

If you can stick to it, exercising at home is one of the most convenient and least time-consuming ways to get fit. If you are serious about getting fit invest in a solid, well made piece of equipment.

Buy from a good sports store which will let you try the equipment before you buy. Try pedalling at different settings and check to see if the flywheel runs smoothly. The cycle should be well balanced and not wobble. It should also be easy to adjust and the controls easy to operate. Digital displays aren't necessarily better and are more likely to break down on cheaper models.

▷ *As with all energetic exercise, stop at regular intervals to top up with water.*

△ *Mountain biking is an excellent, if tough, form of exercise that tones the whole body.*

▽ *Get a fitness assessment at your local gym*

Swimming

Swimming is one of the best and safest forms of aerobic exercise, although it probably doesn't burn as much body fat as running or cycling. Even so it is a fantastic all-over workout and will help strengthen and tone virtually all your muscles as well as improving flexibility.

△ *Start off with a relaxing 10-minute swim, and concentrate on improving your rhythm.*

While you are swimming your body is totally supported by the water and there is very little pressure on the joints. This makes it the best sort of exercise for women who are overweight, injured or pregnant.

Swimming is also ideal for older women and although it doesn't exert any stress on the joints, the pull of the tendons on the bones will still produce some bone-strengthening effect.

The rhythmic strokes of swimming can act as a soothing stress-buster and can help encourage deep breathing – also a potent anti-stress measure.

Technique

◆ Good body alignment is important in all strokes. Make sure you swim with your face in the water and your neck and back in alignment. If you swim with your neck craning out of the water it could cause tension in your neck and aggravate back problems.

◆ Experiment with your arm action. Count how many strokes it takes to cover a length or width. Next time try pulling more strongly with your arms while maintaining your leg action. You should find you can cover the same distance with fewer strokes.

◆ In three strokes – front crawl, back crawl and butterfly – the legs act to steady the body but provide little of the forward thrust. In breast stroke the opposite is true: the powerful leg kick propels the body through the water and is assisted by the arms.

◆ If you are not comfortable with the breathing technique or feel your stroke could be improved, try booking some adult swimming lessons at your local pool. It's never too late to improve your style – or even to start from scratch.

◆ If you don't like getting water in your eyes, invest in a pair of goggles. Anti-fog goggles are best.

Should you swim after a meal?

It's probably wise to wait half an hour before you take a dip. This is because extra blood needed to digest your food will be diverted away from the digestive system to other parts of your body.

◁ *Swimming is a natural 'stress-buster'.*

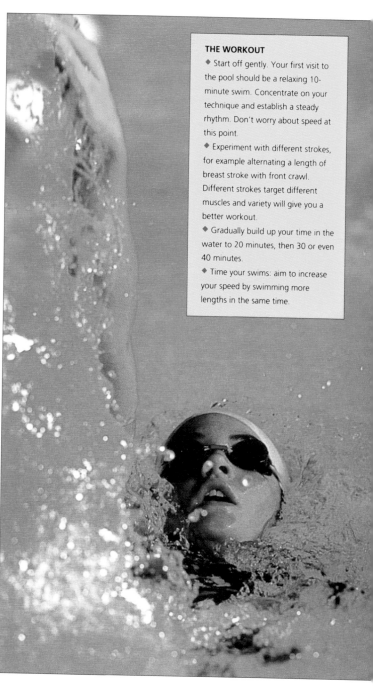

THE WORKOUT

◆ Start off gently. Your first visit to the pool should be a relaxing 10-minute swim. Concentrate on your technique and establish a steady rhythm. Don't worry about speed at this point.

◆ Experiment with different strokes, for example alternating a length of breast stroke with front crawl. Different strokes target different muscles and variety will give you a better workout.

◆ Gradually build up your time in the water to 20 minutes, then 30 or even 40 minutes.

◆ Time your swims: aim to increase your speed by swimming more lengths in the same time.

▽ Weight training will help to strengthen arm and shoulder muscles for swimming.

Step and Aerobics

Aerobics classes can be a lot of fun and are usually great for total body fitness, since a well designed class should include a warm up, cardiovascular section, plus a cool down and stretch. Most classes also include a body conditioning section with excercises for the abdominals and lower body.

Most health clubs these days offer a huge variety of classes from cardiofunk, to step and boxercise. But before you try to work your way through the timetable, ask which classes are best suited to your fitness level. Then try experimenting with a variety of classes until you find out what you enjoy.

◆Don't feel you have to keep up with the rest of the class. Work to your own fitness level.
◆Don't carry on if you are gasping for breath, slow your pace down and walk on the spot. If you stop dead the blood will pool in your legs and you may feel dizzy.
◆Don't jog on your toes make sure you bring your heel down as well. This will reduce your chance of injury.
◆Don't worry if you can't follow complex choreography. Remember lots of the people in the class have been doing the routine for months and sometimes years.
◆If you don't enjoy dance-style classes, experiment with a basic step class or boxercise.
◆If you are overweight or suffer from knee problems, then choose a low impact as opposed to a high impact class.
◆Take regular water breaks.
◆Wear proper aerobics or cross-training shoes to cushion and support your feet.

Step classes

Step aerobics involves, as you might imagine, stepping up and down on a plastic step. If you've never seen a class in action, it sounds odd, but when it was first introduced in 1989, step revolutionized the aerobics industry. People who were bored with their usual classes were suddenly queueing up for step. In, fact step aerobics was so popular some gyms even introduced booking systems for members to reserve places.

Not that it was really anything new – athletes had been running up and down stadium steps for years. So why all the fuss? First of all, compared to running or high impact aerobics, step is a low impact work which means it isn't so stressful for your joints, but at the same time it still provides a tough workout. Secondly, step adds variety, and finally, and probably most importantly: it works. Step really targets hips, thighs and buttocks making them tighter, smaller and well toned. Which is after all, the goal of most women's exercise programmes.

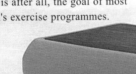

▷ Stand facing your step and step up with your right foot. Follow with your left foot, breathing out as you rise. Now step down backwards with your right foot , and then with your left foot. Continue to repeat the routine with alternating legs, and try to maintain a steady rhythm through your movements. Music can help you to set a pace.

STEPPING SAFETY

◆ Avoid overcrowded step classes – you're more likely to get injured. A good sized class is twenty, but no more. That way the instructor can keep and eye on what everyone is doing.

◆ If you feel the music is too fast to keep up, then it probably is. Some teachers play music so fast that no one has control over their arms and legs. Inevitably, posture suffers and the injury rate soars. So if you don't feel comfortable with the speed, skip the class.

◆ The height of your bench affects workout intensity – the fitter you are the higher you can go. But also • consider your height: short-legged exercisers should never use a high bench since this will put too much stress on the knees and lower back. It's best to stick to 15-20cm (6-8in) steps, any higher and your more likely to hurt yourself.

◆ Foot placement is crucial. Overuse injuries can result from stepping too hard or not placing the foot fully on the step.

◆ Try not to look at your feet as this will throw out your posture and increase your chances of injury.

◆ Don't over do it. Do a maximum of three classes per week.

◆ Avoid handweights or too much arm movement.

△ You should be able to find an aerobics class that suits your fitness level, and that you enjoy.

Using a Gym

Don't be put off going to a gym because you are unfit or feel you are overweight. Of course, some women there will be superfit – with Barbie Doll bodies, but they are in the minority.

Many people find it easier to exercise in a health club, because they enjoy the social atmosphere and prefer to exercise with other people. It's also useful to have trained instructors on hand to help with your fitness programme.

Joining a gym or health club will only help you get fit if you actually go, and they're usually expensive, so make sure you do your homework before you pay the membership fee. A good club will let prospective clients look around before they join. They may even allow you to join for a trial day before you commit to a full membership. Here's what to look for:

◆ Is the gym convenient? Is it near where you live or work? If not, is it on a convenient route? Going to the gym is hard enough, so the location should make it easy to visit.
◆ Does it have the facilities you are looking for? More expensive clubs may have swimming pools, sauna and steam rooms, but will you use these facilities often enough to make the extra expense worth while? One recent survey found that many people join health clubs for the pool, but in reality most used it only rarely.
◆ Check that all the instructors are qualified.

△ *Joining a health club can be expensive, so make sure that it meets your specific needs.*

◆ Visit the gym and ask to be shown around. Make sure you see the health club at about the time of day you plan to use it and check to see how crowded the gym and changing rooms are.
◆ Check the class timetable: does it fit in with your schedule? There should be a number of different classes on offer at times that suit you – that way you won't get bored.
◆ What is the atmosphere like? Do you feel comfortable with the type of people? Some clubs are geared up to body-building men, others are very upmarket, others are more down to earth. Choose a place that meets your needs.

◁ *A well-equipped gym will have a good range of facilities, for every level of fitness.*

◆ Is the club well kept? Check to see if the changing rooms are clean and the equipment is well maintained.

The Equipment

You will usually find three different types of equipment in any gym or health club. First there are the cardiovascular (CV) machines such as stationary bikes, stair climbing machines, cross-country ski machines, rowers and treadmills.

The best club models tend to give digital displays and offer a number of different programmes. Make sure the club you join has enough CV equipment to go around, as people tend to use these for longer – 20 or more minutes at a time – and queueing can be very frustrating.

Resistance Training

Then there is resistance equipment: machines built to enhance a strength training programme. They are usually easier to control than free weights. Free weights – dumbbells and barbells – are usually used by more advanced exercisers, although there is no reason why beginners shouldn't use them providing they are properly supervised.

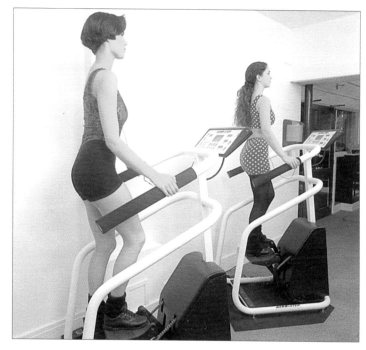

△ Stair climbing machines offer excellent cardiovascular (CV) exercise, combined with computerized training programmes tailored to suit your own requirements.

▽ There are many different types of resistance training machines, but they are all designed to allow controlled, precise exercise and toning of particular groups of muscles.

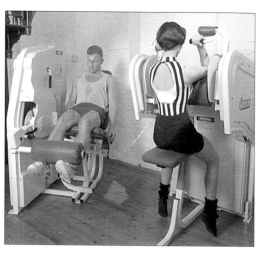

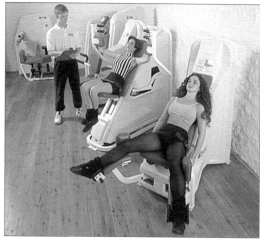

Adolescence

Young women today appear to be maturing earlier than ever before.
By the age of 13 the typical adolescent girl will already be
menstruating and may be physically very developed.

Some girls start to menstruate by the age of 10, though others don't start until 15 or 16. It's important for both mother and daughter to realize these variations are perfectly normal.

Body image and weight gain

The process of becoming a woman can be an ordeal. As children, boys and girls have very similar bodies, but as girls grow up their long straight bodies develop womanly breasts, stomach and hips. Just before this they also shoot up in height.

Over a period of four years the average girl will become 25 per cent taller and almost double her body weight. Most girls find these changes disconcerting. Often they don't want to change and are embarrassed by their developing bodies.

It's also normal for girls to gain a lot of weight very quickly. Not surprisingly, in our weight-obsessed society, this development is usually unwelcome. Some girls gain extra body fat before they grow taller, but this isn't the time to start a diet; extra puppy fat will usually disappear when they shoot up.

Research indicates that it is these girls who are most vulnerable to anorexia. About one per cent of adolescent girls become anorexic and another two to three per cent develop bulimia   binge

▷ *Girls often find adolescence an ordeal as their bodies develop into womanhood.*

eating and purging. But these statistics refer to severe clinical conditions and the true incidence is probably much more widespread.

If you suspect a teenage girl has an eating disorder, speak to her about it – otherwise you are condoning her behaviour. If she won't talk to you, try providing the names and numbers of specialist counsellors. Also remember mothers are powerful role models. If you have an adolescent daughter try not to skip meals or constantly focus on your own weight. Every time you groan about your hips or thighs a young girl will look at hers and think, 'mine are no better'.

Sadly, teenage girls are much more likely to be unhappy about their bodies than boys. They may change their clothes several times before they decide what to wear – they are not being vain, only uncomfortable with the way they look.

During this rapid growth spurt, girls may need to sleep more than usual – some parents put this down to teenage laziness, but the body produces more growth hormones during sleep. If you have a constantly hungry teenager in the house, stock up with healthy nutritious snacks and avoid buying junk food.

What girls need to know

Girls who cope best with the changes of puberty are usually the best informed. This is where mothers can play an important role in explaining the changes which are about to take place. An ongoing discussion between mother and daughter should begin at around the age of nine, before the hormonal changes begin. It's best if the mother can think of an easy way to explain the biology herself, rather than giving her daughter a book.

Later when the mother notices the first signs of puberty such as developing breasts and pubic hair she should pick up the subject again. In fact the girls who are most at ease with their bodies grow up in homes where their father knows when they have started to menstruate and they can talk to both parents openly.

Adolescence is a time of change, which often brings with it stress – related to appearance, friendships, school work and the opposite sex.

Contraception

The choice of contraception has never been so good, but how do you know which is right for you? The answer will be influenced by your age, health and lifestyle, but at the end of the day it comes down to personal choice.

There are three main types: hormonal, barrier methods and intra-uterine devices (IUDs). Each has pros and cons.

HORMONAL METHODS

THE COMBINED PILL

This contains the hormones oestrogen and progestogen. It works by preventing ovulation and encouraging the cervical mucus to thicken and form a barrier to the sperm. It also alters the movement of the fallopian tubes to slow the journey of the sperm towards the egg and thins the lining of the womb to make it less receptive.

Normally a course is taken over 21 days with a seven day break before starting the next pack, but it also comes in a 28-day pack with seven dummy pills.

Pros: many women find the pill the most convenient form of contraception. Other advantages include protection against certain diseases such as ovarian cancer, ovarian cysts, endometriosis, anaemia, polycystic ovaries, benign breast tumours and heavy or painful periods.

Cons: modern pills contain far lower doses of hormones than they did in the 1960s, with fewer side-effects and health risks. But still, if you smoke or are overweight you should stop taking the pill at 35. The pill may increase the risk of some illnesses especially if they run in the family. It increases the risk of heart disease and strokes in smokers. It is also associated with a slightly higher risk of thrombosis (blood clot in a vein) high blood pressure and, in women under 35, breast cancer.

▽ *Many couples find that the 'pill' is a convenient, effective and trouble-free method of contraception.*

Reliability: used carefully the combined pill is 99 per cent effective: if 100 couples use it for a year only one woman will get pregnant. It should be taken at the same time every day and is not effective if taken more than 12 hours late.

The worst pills to miss are at the beginning and end of each packet. If you do miss a pill, take it as soon as you remember, and if you missed more than one take the most recent one you missed. If you are more than 12 hours late you should use another form of contraception as well for the next seven days.

If the missed pill was one of the last seven in the packet, take the pill as before while using another method of contraception for seven days and start the next packet immediately – skipping the pill-free week. You will get a bleed at the end of the second packet.

The pill won't work if you are sick within three hours of swallowing it or if you have severe diarrhoea within 12 hours – again you should use another form of contraception. Some prescription drugs will also interfere with the pill's action, so check with your doctor how long you will be unprotected.

THE PROGESTOGEN-ONLY PILL

Also known as the mini pill, it only contains one hormone: progestogen. These pills are taken every day with no breaks between packets and work by thickening the mucus at the neck of the womb, making it difficult for the sperm to enter.

Pros: it can be used by women who are advised against the combined pill, such as smokers, breast-feeding mothers and women over 40.

Cons: it must be taken at the same time every day and is not effective taken

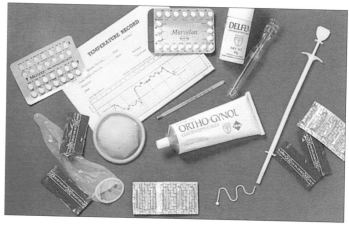

▷ *It is important to take the 'mini pill' at the same time each day, as it is not effective if it is taken more than three hours late.*

more than three hours late. If you do miss a pill, take it as soon as you remember even if it means taking two in one day – and use another form of contraception for the next seven days.

The mini pill can cause spotting or irregular periods, but these problems are usually resolved quickly. It is not suitable for women weighing over 70 kg (150lb).

Reliability: used carefully it is 99 per cent effective.

△ *The choice of a suitable method of contraception will be influenced by your age and medical history, as well as being a matter of personal preference. There are many reliable forms of contraception for you to assess before making a decision.*

Implants

These are small tubes placed under the skin which release hormones into the blood stream. They can be left in place for five years and work in the same way as the pill, but without the problem of missed pills. Insertion can be painful.

Injectables

These work in the same way as the pill, but the effect lasts for three months. Some women complain of weight gain, loss of sex drive and acne.

Emergency contraception

If you have taken a risk, emergency contraception is available from your doctor and is effective up to 72 hours after intercourse. There are two options: either two doses of two high-dose contraceptive pills, taken 12 hours apart. Or an IUD, which stops the fertilized egg from implanting in the womb.

▽ *Variety is the spice of life – and when it comes to condoms there are a wealth of colours and textures to select from. Condoms are 98 per cent effective when used correctly.*

▷ *If you are considering using a diaphragm or cap, you will need to visit your doctor or family planning centre for an internal examination to be fitted for the correct size.*

BARRIER METHODS

These work by preventing the sperm meeting the egg. Caps, diaphragms and condoms also protect against sexually transmitted diseases and women who use them are less likely to contract pre-cancerous cervical changes or cancer of the cervix.

CONDOMS

It's worth trying different brands as they vary slightly in size and shape – Durex Gold are slightly longer, for example.

Pros: condoms are the only reversible form of contraception where the man takes some responsibility. Used properly they offer the best protection against HIV and other sexually transmitted disease.

Cons: some men find them uncomfortable and some people are allergic to latex, although Durex now makes the Allergy Condom.

Reliability: condoms are 98 per cent effective used correctly. You need to put on the condom before the penis enters the vagina, since some sperm naturally leak out before ejaculation. The man must pull out of the woman before he loses his erection in case the condom slips off. He must always hold the base of the condom as he pulls out, as this will stop any spillage which could make you pregnant.

DIAPHRAGMS AND CAPS

These names are often used interchangeably, although in fact they are not the same thing. Diaphragms are larger and consist of rubber over a flexible metal ring. Caps are smaller, thimble-like and made entirely of rubber.

Both devices fit over the neck of the womb and act as a barrier to sperm. They are more effective if used with spermicide which helps prevent pregnancy by killing the sperm. They must be left in place for six hours after lovemaking.

You can obtain a cap or diaphragm from your doctor or family planning clinic and will need an internal examination to be fitted for size.

Pros: they offer some protection from sexually transmitted diseases. Both can be inserted well before love-making, but if you wait more than three hours you must use extra spermicide just before sex.

Cons: they take some practice to insert properly and so have a higher failure rate early on. Some men complain they can feel the rim of the diaphragm during love-making and some women have problems with cystitis.

Reliability: used carefully they are 92–96 per cent effective.

IUD

The intra-uterine device (IUD) or coil is a small T-shaped plastic and copper device which is fitted in the womb by a doctor or nurse. The IUD works by changing the biochemical balance of the uterus, making it unreceptive to the fertilized egg. Some researchers believe it prevents fertilization taking place at all.

Pros: the IUD can be left in place for five years and if fitted after the age of 40 can be left in place until the menopause.

Cons: it can cause heavy periods and slightly increases the risk of an ectopic pregnancy (a pregnancy in the fallopian tube which requires emergency treatment and removal of the tube).

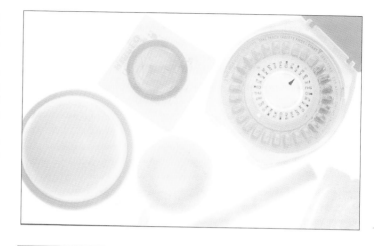

CONDOM SENSE

◆ Putting on two male condoms does not make it twice as safe and may actually increase the chance of the condom breaking as they rub against each other.

◆ Don't use baby oil or any other oil-based lubricant as this will destroy the condom and make it break.

If the woman is exposed to infection she will be more likely to pick up the disease since the coil acts as a ladder, helping the germs to climb up into the womb. This means it is only suitable for monogamous couples.

▽ *Reliable contraception will ensure that your lovemaking is worry-free.*

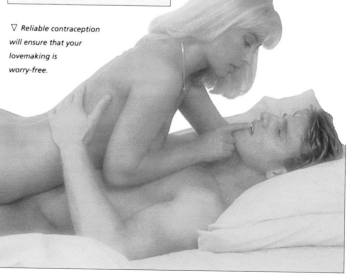

Sexual Health

Millions of people every year are infected by a sexually transmitted disease. Like coughs, colds and flu they are simply infections and nothing to be ashamed of. But unlike colds and coughs the implications can range from minor, to deadly – as in the case of AIDS.

△ *Condoms are the safest form of protection.*

Sexually transmitted diseases (STDs) are very common, statistics show one in every five women of child-bearing age in America has an STD. Most will clear up for good with the appropriate treatment, but others have more serious long term consequences for our health. Women in particular need to protect themselves. Firstly, because when they come into contact with an STD they are more likely to become infected than a man – the cervix (neck of the womb) is a warm, receptive breeding ground.

Secondly, because left unchecked the long term health consequences can be

△ *Sensible precautions can help to keep you free from sexually transmitted disease.*

devastating – including pelvic inflammatory disease (PID), ectopic pregnancy, increased risk of cervical cancer and sterility. What's worrying is you might have an STD and not even realize. Some infections can go on for years without symptoms, so it's important to go for regular check-ups.

Infections triggered by bacteria and parasites can be treated easily by taking the appropriate drugs. These include chlamydia, gonorrhea, syphilis and trichomonas. But other infections which are caused by viruses – such HIV, herpes, hepatitis B and the human papilloma virus (HPV), which causes genital warts, can not be cured, although their symptoms may be treated successfully.

Who is most at risk?

Women who are under 25 with multiple partners – or who have partners with multiple partners without using protection are most at risk. Multiple short term relationships – even monogamous ones – put the woman in a high-risk category unless she also takes steps to protect herself. Your partner's sexual history is also relevant. The more people he has had sex with the riskier unprotected sex with him will be.

If your partner complains of burning when passing water this is likely to

indicate an STD, whereas serious STDS such as chlamydia and gonorrhea almost never cause symptoms in women.

Women are more vulnerable than men because the lining of the cervix is more receptive to infection than the penis. Intercourse is also more likely to cause abrasions and trauma, leaving the womb even more vulnerable to infection. Plus the woman comes into contact with more fluid from the ejaculation than a man does from vaginal fluid.

What can a woman do to protect herself?

Condoms – both the male and the newer female variety – are your best protection against any sexually transmitted disease.

Make sure the brand used states it will protect against STDs. Not all brands can be counted on, so look out for the British Standards Kitemark.

They are especially effective against diseases passed on in bodily fluids like HIV, chlamydia and gonorrhea. One study published in the *New England Journal of Medicine* followed 300 couples where one partner had HIV. Following 15,000 separate encounters where condoms were used there wasn't one case of HIV transmission.

Condoms are less effective at protecting against diseases passed on by skin-to-skin contact like herpes, syphilis and HPV. Nor do they offer any protection from scabies or crabs.

Spermicides do contain chemicals which breakdown and destroy some STDs, but they may also act as an irritant increasing the chances of sores and inflammation, thus making a woman more vulnerable to infection. So no claims can be made for the protective effects of spermicides as yet.

Is it possible to catch an STD from oral sex?

Yes, it is. Experts say you should use a condom every time you have sex whether it is vaginal, anal or oral. But in reality few people do.

Oral sex is less risky, but most experts agree it is not absolutely safe. The disease least likely to be passed on by oral sex is HIV, because the saliva carries little of the virus and semen and vaginal secretions carry less than blood. Giving oral sex to a woman is a lot less risky than giving oral sex to a man. The main risk comes from the ejaculation into the mouth and remember some fluid is always released before the actual orgasm. Chlamydia, NSU and gonorrhea can also be transmitted via oral sex although there's very little evidence that they can be caught by giving oral sex to a woman. Genital warts can be transmitted to the mouth but this is very rare.

Herpes is more likely to be passed on during oral sex. If you have a cold sore and you give someone oral sex the chances of giving them genital herpes are quite high. The increased rate of herpes maybe explained by the increased popularity of oral sex and cold sores being passed on from the lips to genitals.

Can I catch an STD by touching and kissing?

Herpes can be passed on by kissing, as for example in oral sex.

Kissing and touching are considered very low risk for other diseases including the AIDs virus. Warts on your hands are a different strain to genital warts and aren't passed on by touching the genitals.

What STD is most likely to threaten my fertility?

Chlamydia, is one of the most common STDs, but it is often symptomless and least likely to be detected. In the long term it can lead to infertility, so it is important for every woman to go for regular checks, if she has had unprotected sex. Left untreated 20% of cases of chlamydia develop into pelvic inflammatory infection which can cause infertility. It's also important to get your partner treated too, to avoid re-infection.

▽ *Some viruses can be passed on by kissing, but, generally, there is little risk of infection.*

WARNING SIGNS

◆ Itching can be a sign of crabs, but can also be a sign of a vaginal infection like thrush (which is not an STD) or a skin condition like psoriasis.

◆ Burning pain while urinating could indicate herpes, gonorrhea or chlamydia, but it could also be the result of a urinary tract infection like cystitis which can be treated with antibiotics.

◆ A change in vaginal discharge.

◆ A sore spot.

◆ Recurrent dull pelvic pain.

Perfect Pregnancy

Some women get pregnant as soon as they start trying for a baby, others take longer and the average time to conceive is four months. Women are most fertile in their early twenties and fertility declines rapidly after the age of thirty-five. Even so, the patterns of motherhood are changing and more and more women are choosing to leave pregnancy until later.

Whenever you choose to have your baby, it makes sense to plan your pregnancy because you can improve your chances of having a healthy baby.

It makes sense to moderate your behaviour three months before you start trying for a baby. Some of the most crucial stages of development take place in the first few weeks of pregnancy, before you even know you're pregnant, so doctors advise any woman who is trying to conceive to consider herself pregnant the week before her period is due and avoid anything which has been linked to birth defects.

What will happen to my body?
During pregnancy your body and hormone levels go through dramatic changes. Even before you look pregnant a surge in hormone levels can make you feel strange. Some women feel miserable, others feel fabulous and others swing between the two.

You're also likely to feel more tired and emotional than usual and may experience minor health problems such as breast tenderness, nausea, constipation, back ache and water retention.

▽ *Most women can carry on with physical activities without any ill effect during their pregnancy. Yoga is excellent for relaxing and exercising the expectant mother, and is beneficial in maintaining a toned and flexible body.*

△ *Due to the hormonal surges during pregnancy, many women swing between feeling on top of the world to feeling thoroughly miserable.*

BEFORE YOU GET PREGNANT

◆Stop smoking. Smokers' babies weigh less, which adversely affects their development.

◆Stop drinking alcohol. Excess alcohol can lead to growth deficiencies, delayed mental development, poor co-ordination and muscle strength which persist through childhood.

◆Avoid recreational drugs.

◆Stop dieting. Low-calorie diets may not provide the essential nutrients needed for a developing baby.

◆Take a folic acid supplement. This will reduce your chances of having a baby with a central nervous system defect such as spina bifida.

◆Check your immunity against rubella with your doctor. This will require a simple blood test. If you are not protected you can have a vaccination, but must then continue to use contraception for the next three months. Catching the disease in the first three months of pregnancy can damage a baby's hearing, eyesight, heart and mental development.

Nausea
When will I get it?
From two weeks after the first missed period until week 14.
What can I do about it?
Eat small, frequent meals.

Breast tenderness
When will I get it?
In the first few months
What can I do about it?
Wear a supportive bra.

Constipation
When will I get it?
After the first three months.
What can I do to help it?
Eat plenty of fibre.

Fatigue
When will I get it?
Especially in the first and last three months, but all through pregnancy.
What can I do to help it?
Make time for extra rest periods.

Fluid retention
When will I get it?
A small amount of fluid retention is normal from the fifth month on. You should see a doctor if there is a sudden increase in swelling, you're going to the lavatory less often than normal or the swelling is accompanied by a headache.
What can I do to help it?
Surprisingly, drink plenty of water.

Backache
When will I get it?
Throughout pregnancy, but especially in the last three months
What can I do to help it?
Pay attention to your posture and avoid wearing high heels.

◁ *The developing baby can experience many sensations, and reacts to its mother's emotions.*

The Menopause

The menopause marks the end of a woman's child-bearing years and usually occurs between the ages of 45 and 55, although it may occur as early as 40 – or even earlier, in which case it is known as premature menopause. Over the years the ovaries have released most of the eggs and as they shut down, the hormones oestrogen and progesterone decline.

A woman's periods may suddenly stop or they may become irregular. The change can be abrupt or it may last a number of months or even years. Most women experience symptoms caused by the reduced or fluctuating oestrogen levels such as hot flushes, night sweats, thinning and drying of the skin, thinning hair, breast changes, loss of sexual desire and vaginal dryness – although 20 per cent experience no symptoms at all.

A woman may also experience mood swings, tiredness, poor memory, irritability and lack of concentration. These may be caused by hormone fluctuations, but may also be due to the stress caused by menopause symptoms.

In Western cultures we tend to regard the menopause as a negative event, which exacerbates the symptoms, whereas other cultures celebrate menopause as a liberating event in a woman's life. In Sub-Saharan Africa and Ethiopia post-menopausal women are given great respect and status, while in the West we worship everything youthful, so it's no wonder menopause makes many women miserable.

Long-term health

After the menopause women lose the protective effect of oestrogen and become more vulnerable to osteoporosis (thinning, brittle bones), heart disease and strokes.

Hormone Replacement Therapy

Hormone Replacement Therapy (HRT), prescribed by your doctor, will replace the oestrogen lost after menopause and can help reduce many of the symptoms.

On the plus side, HRT can help protect against osteoporosis, heart disease and cancers of the cervix, endometrium and ovaries. It can also help women keep their pre-menopausal figure – after menopause women become more apple-shaped, gaining fat around the midriff rather than on their hips. HRT can also

◁ *Regular exercise, such as swimming, will help to reduce some of the side-effects of the menopause and improve your general health.*

◁ Hormone Replacement Therapy (HRT) will assist you to keep your figure and protect against osteoporosis, heart disease and some cancers, as well as helping you lead a full life.
▷ Use this period of your life to make time for yourself and to develop new interests.

reduce the loss of collagen and prevent thinning of the skin and hair which can occur after menopause.

Some forms of HRT contain testosterone as well as oestrogen and progestogen, which can really improve a woman's sex drive.

SELF-HELP REMEDIES

◆ Herbal remedies such fenugreek, gotu kola, ginseng, sarsaparilla, liquorice root and tan kwai (or dong quai) may help to reduce hot flushes.
◆ Chamomile tea may help with relaxation.
◆ Cut down on smoking – the first puff on each cigarette can trigger a hot flush.
◆ Sleep on a towel – this will absorb the water from night sweats.
◆ Take lukewarm showers rather than baths.
◆ Reduce caffeine and alcohol intake.
◆ Vitamin E can help reduce sweating and flushes. Take 200–400 iu (international units) each day. It will take three to four weeks to see an effect.
◆ Regular exercise will reduce intensity and frequency of flushes. It will also reduce your risk of heart disease and brittle bones.
◆ Cut back on the fat in your diet and make sure you are eating enough vitamin-rich fruit and vegetables. This will reduce the likelihood of heart disease and stop you gaining weight.

Unfortunately, as with most drugs, there are side-effects, which include the return of monthly bleeds and premenstrual-type symptoms such as bloating, weight gain, breast tenderness and menstrual cramps. Side-effects usually settle after two months. Switching to a different type of progestogen or changing the delivery method (creams, patches, implants or pills) may also help, so if you find the side-effects unacceptable you should see your doctor.

New developments include no-bleed HRT – the hormones are taken with no break, although the long-term effects of this treatment are not yet known.

HRT may slightly increase your chances of developing breast cancer, possibly by stimulating an existing tumour to develop. It may also make fibroids, endometriosis or gallstones worse.

HRT is not recommended for women who are diabetic, have high blood pressure or have a history of endometriosis, fibroids or gallstones – though they may find patches or implants more suitable than pills. HRT in any form is not suitable for women with a past history of breast cancer, cancer of the endometrium, heart disease, severe liver or kidney disease, and otosclerosis (oestrogen-related hearing loss).

△ A simple programme of gentle, stretching exercises will increase your heart rate and relax your muscles. A regular fitness workout will also help to strengthen bones and reduce the effects of osteoporosis.

A Good Night's Sleep

We spend a third of our lives asleep. Psychologists aren't sure why we sleep, but we are genetically programmed so that we do. Most people need about seven to eight hours a night although some feel fine on as little as four hours sleep.

Sleep restores us both physically and psychologically and as mothers with young babies will testify, a night of interrupted sleep makes us feel tired, irritable and unable to concentrate the next day. Even as little as two hours' sleep deprivation can cause poor concentration – about 10 per cent of traffic accidents are sleep-related. Several recent disasters, including the nuclear disaster at Chernobyl, have been blamed on workers falling asleep. It's worrying then, that so many people complain they get less sleep than they need.

▽ *Sleep is a time of replenishment and repair.*

Insomnia

One in three people have problems sleeping – twice as many women as men. It's not clear why more women suffer although it may be due to hormonal influences. But if you are having problems, think twice before turning to sleeping pills. If you do use them try to rely on them only in the short term. Sleeping pills do not induce normal, refreshing sleep, which is an active, positive phase of mental activity. Instead they induce a semi-coma which is almost useless in providing real rest and mental problem-solving.

There are a number of different stages to sleep and we move through several cycles a night. The deeper stages of sleep are thought to be a time for growth and repair, while dreaming is thought to be psychologically refreshing – helping us to sort and file our thoughts and information.

Babies sleep up to 18 hours a day, whereas pensioners may sleep less than six. The quality of sleep is different too. The younger we are the more time we spend in deep stage four sleep, while old people sleep lightly and spend more time in the shallow dozing stages of sleep.

Deep sleep is physically replenishing. The body pours out growth hormones and repairs all its cells. Some experts have even speculated that long-term sleep deprivation will lead to premature ageing.

Some aspects of the immune system

△ We pass through a number of cycles of different depth during a night's sleep.

▽ If you can't get to sleep, relax in a warm bath with a few drops of lavender oil.

HOW TO ENSURE THAT YOU GET A GOOD NIGHT'S SLEEP

◆ Make sure there's enough fresh air in your bedroom.

◆ Exercise can help you relax and sleep, but do your workout several hours before you plan to sleep. Early evening or late afternoon is best.

◆ Try not to eat late at night – this will fire up your metabolism at a time when you should be winding down.

◆ Cut back on coffee.

◆ Don't eat or read in bed. Reserve your bed for sleeping and your mind will start to associate it with sleep.

◆ If you can't sleep, don't lie there tossing and turning. Get up and do something else until you are tired.

◆ Soak in a warm bath with a few drops of lavender oil. Lavender oil has been shown to be just as effective as sleeping pills in helping people fall asleep, and it does not interfere with the natural sleep process in the way sleeping pills do.

◆ Other home remedies include: a teaspoon of honey 20 minutes before bed, warm milk spiced with nutmeg, or camomile tea.

◆ As you get older, don't expect to sleep as much.

---

are enhanced during sleep: shift workers who tend to sleep poorly get more infections than the rest of us, though this could also be blamed on the stress of disrupted daily rhythms.

Lack of sleep may also contribute to weight gain and overeating. One study of nurses found that 90 per cent gained weight while working shifts. Possibly because one of the chemicals we produce during sleep helps suppress appetite, but more likely because tired hands grab the easiest energy fix: sweet sugary snacks which are high in calories and fat.

Eating Disorders

In a society which places such high value on being slim, many women have a tortured relationship with food and their bodies. Sadly, eating disorders are rife, particularly among teenage girls.

On top of the official figures – one per cent of young women suffer from anorexia, two per cent bulimia and two per cent binge-eating disorder – there are many hidden or borderline cases, such as women who follow strict diets by periods of bingeing. This kind of eating pattern is so common that many women consider it normal, or at least inevitable.

What causes eating disorders?

Pinpointing the exact cause of an eating disorder is impossible. A woman's obsession with food may start at any time. It may be when she is teased by her classmates for being chubby, or when she notices her thighs are bigger than her friends'.

Women who suffer from eating disorders tend to be perfectionists and at the same time suffer from low self-esteem. Eating disorders may be a symptom of other emotional problems or strained family relationships and food may be the one thing they feel they can control in their lives.

Often women use their bodies as a focus for their unhappiness and the fact that slim equals beautiful in our society certainly encourages the problem.

Sadly bulimics, who binge then purge by vomiting or taking handfuls of laxatives, destroy their health and their looks. Constant vomiting erodes the enamel on their teeth and makes the

glands swell, so their faces actually appear chubbier. And while handfuls of laxatives will give them stomach cramps, they have no effect on their calorie intake. Calories are absorbed higher in the gut, while laxatives affect the lower intestine. Vomiting can only expel a half to a third of what has been eaten, so bingers still absorb lots of calories.

▷ *Many adolescents and women suffer from eating disorders such as bulimia and anorexia, which may be symptoms of emotional problems or strained relationships.*

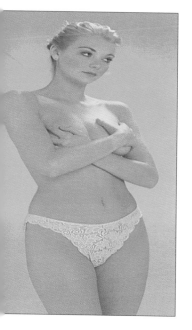

△ Try to reduce cravings for sugary junk food by planning healthy, regular meals.
◁ Many teenage girls have distorted images of their bodies and believe they are too fat, leading to problems with eating disorders.
▽ If you think that you have an eating disorder, talk to a friend who can help you to get professional help from a doctor or trained therapist.

Anorexics who refuse to eat literally starve themselves. Some will be hospitalized until they have gained weight and tragically some will die. Anorexia is difficult to treat, especially since most anorexics have distorted body images and really believe they are still too fat.

If you have an eating disorder

◆ Don't keep your problem to yourself. You may feel ashamed and disgusted but it's important to seek help.
◆ Eating disorders are best helped by a professional therapist, so ask your doctor for a referral.

Self-help for compulsive eating

◆ People who binge find they no longer know how to eat normally. Try to organize three regular meals and two snacks a day. Plan what time you will eat these and stick to the times. Regular meals will reduce your urge to binge and gradually normal sensations of hunger and fullness will return.

◆ When you feel the urge to binge do something else instead. Take a shower, go for a walk, call a friend. Continue this activity until the urge passes. Don't be disheartened if you don't always succeed.
◆ Monitor your problem and try to work out what triggers your binges. Do you binge when you are tired, bored, angry or upset? What would be a better way of dealing with these feelings?
◆ Do you follow very strict diets, then binge when you can't keep to them? If the answer is yes, stop dieting in this way. It may take two or three months to get out of the habit, but it is worth persisting.
◆ Do certain foods trigger binges? Gradually introduce these foods into your diet on days when you feel in control. Focus on the easiest foods for two weeks, then gradually introduce others. After about eight weeks you should have eaten all your trigger foods. You don't have to eat these foods regularly – only until the thought of eating them no longer disturbs you.

Looking After Your Breasts

Considering their importance as a symbol of female sexuality and beauty, it's surprising how little attention most women actually pay to their breasts. Breasts are made up entirely of glandular tissue and fat. Since they contain no muscle, there is little we can do to alter their size and shape. However, strengthening the pectoral muscles on which they rest can give your breasts a natural lift and regular aerobic exercise may reduce your risk of developing breast cancer.

Breast awareness is vital because early diagnosis increases the likelihood of a cure. Ninety per cent of breast lumps are found by women or their partners. One in three women will find a lump at some point in their lives and in nine out of 10 cases it won't be cancer, but it should still be investigated by a doctor.

Breast Examination

Breast examination should be done once a month, two or three days after your period. But it should not take the place of regular mammograms.

In the shower

Raise your left arm. With the flat part of your fingers on your right hand, carefully examine your left breast. Starting from the outer top of your breast press firmly in a circular motion around the breast. After one full circle, move 2.5cm (1in) further in and repeat again, continuing until you reach the nipple. Check the area above the breast, especially the armpit, for lumps or hard knots.

▷ *Check your breasts in a mirror – first with hands at your sides, then behind your head.*

In front of a mirror

Place your hands at your sides and check breasts for any changes in shape, colour, size or dimpling or scaling of the skin. Check again with your hands clasped behind your head.

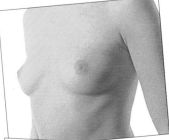

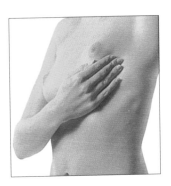

△ *Start from the outer top of your breast.*

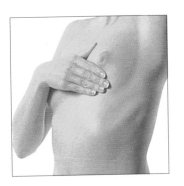

△ *Press around the breast in a circular motion.*

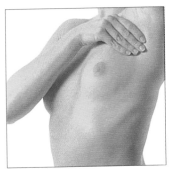

△ *Finally, check your armpit area for lumps.*

Lying down

With a pillow under your left shoulder, raise your left hand above your head. Examine the whole of your breast in a circular motion. Repeat on your right breast. Squeeze each nipple gently to check for discharge.

Check for changes

If one of your nipples starts to turn inwards or develops a scaly rash, tell your doctor. These could be early warning signs of breast cancer.

Breast Protection

◆ Use a high-factor sunscreen on delicate chest skin.

◆ Avoid rapid weight gain or loss as this stretches the delicate breast tissue and causes sagging.

◆ Examine your breasts every month, after your period, when they are least tender.

◆ Many women wear the wrong size bra – up to 70 per cent of us, in fact. Ask a professional fitter in a good department store to measure you before you buy your next bra. Remember your bra size may change if you gain or lose weight. If you are wearing the right size, the underband will be firm, but comfortable. If it is too loose the back will ride up. Too small and it will dig in leaving red marks. Each breast should feel well supported and reach the end of the cup with no over-spill.

◆ Premenstrual breast pain may be helped by a supplement containing GLA (gamma-linolenic acid) such as evening primrose oil or starflower oil.

◆ Your diet can also reduce your risk of breast cancer. Make sure you eat at least five portions of fruit and vegetables a day – these contain the anti-oxidant vitamins C, E and beta carotene, which protect against cancer. You should also reduce your intake of animal fats, especially red meat, which has been linked to increased risk of breast cancer.

◆ Several studies have found that breast-feeding over several pregnancies or for several months at a time reduces the risk of breast cancer.

◆ Keep your weight within the recommended guidelines. If you start to put weight on your stomach take steps to lose weight, but without crash dieting. Apple-shaped women have a slightly increased risk of breast cancer than those who are pear-shaped.

△ *Lay down with a pillow under one shoulder and raise that arm above your head. With the other hand, examine the whole of your breast in a circular motion. Repeat on your other breast. Check with your doctor if you discover any lumps – but remember that in nine out of 10 cases, a lump will not be linked to cancer.*

▽ *Mammograms can detect tiny breast tumours early, however, regular exposure to the X-rays used may not be desirable.*

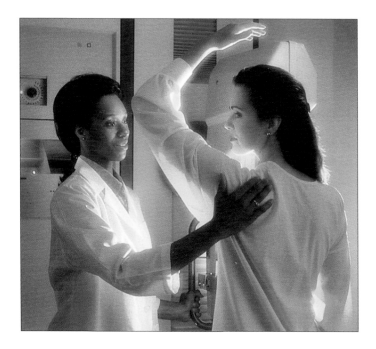

Healthy Hair

Everyone wants to see a glossy, healthy head of hair when they look in the mirror. But few of us are satisfied with the hair we've got. If we're blessed with a halo of wild curls we want straight hair and if our tresses are dead straight we long for waves.

The majority of hair problems we experience, such as drying, splitting and frizzing, can be blamed on our attempts to change our natural type and colour.

Chemical processing such as colouring and perming dries and damages the hair, leaving it weakened and prone to breaking. Overbrushing roughens the hair cuticle making it look dull rather than shiny. Holding a drier too close to the hair can dry or even burn it.

Well-conditioned hair requires as much restraint as attention. Over-treating it will ruffle the outer cuticle, making it look dull. It also makes the hair more porous, allowing substances to creep in and ruin the condition further.

Washing and conditioning

Washing your hair every day won't do it any harm, although it probably isn't necessary unless your hair is greasy. If you do, some hairdressers recommend simply shampooing the scalp and avoiding the ends. Only one application of shampoo is necessary. If you're on a budget, invest in a good shampoo and spend less on the conditioner, since some cheap brands strip the hair of its natural moisture.

Short hair does not need a conditioner every day, even if it is dry. Your hair has the ability to condition itself. So even a light water-based conditioner only needs to be used a couple of times a week on normal hair and three times a week on dry hair. If you have long tresses, use a conditioner every time you wash your hair but only on the ends where it's needed.

Losing hair

It is normal to lose between 50-100 hairs every day. Every three months there may be a period of increased shedding in preparation for new growth. Symptoms of true hair loss or alopecia include bald patches, a receding hairline or losing handfuls rather than strands.

This severe kind of hair loss is often linked to hormonal changes such as at the menopause; stress and illness; or a diet lacking in protein, iron or vitamins.

If you are suffering from thinning hair, you should see a doctor to determine the cause. HRT can help reduce hair thinning at menopause.

Health, diet and your hair

There are numerous styling, glossing and colouring products, all designed to make your hair look thicker or glossier, but nothing will affect the look of your hair so much as your general health.

Hair cells grow faster than practically any other part of the body and require a continuous supply of nutrients. But because hair is not essential it is low down

◁ *Lustrous hair requires a steady supply of nutrients that can be found in a healthy diet.*

the body's list of priorities. When nutrients are scarce our hair is the first to show it. It's no coincidence when a woman who diets throughout her pregnancy finds her hair is lank and thin, or when an anorexic girl's malnourished hair becomes dull and eventually falls out. Even everyday diets or skipping meals will deprive the hair follicles of nutrients, causing poor condition. Eat a well balanced diet including plenty of fruit and vegetables.

DAMAGE CONTROL

◆ Take care when your hair is wet as it loses much of its elasticity and is prone to breaking.

◆ Use the hair drier on a warm rather than hot setting.

◆ Blow-dry in downward strokes to keep the cuticle flat and looking glossy.

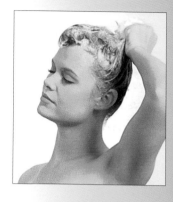

△ If you have long hair use a conditioner only on the ends where it is needed.

△ Hair loses much of its elasticity when it is wet, so take care that you do not damage it.

△ Unless you have greasy hair you won't have to wash it every day. Use one application of shampoo and use conditioner sparingly. Blow-dry your hair in downward strokes, using a warm, rather than hot, setting.

Skin Care

No other part of the body comes under such close scrutiny as the skin. In our beauty-obsessed society many women bake on the beach to obtain a desirable golden glow – yet we are constantly searching for ways to fend off wrinkles. We spend a fortune on expensive creams and increasingly turn to cosmetic surgery to iron out the evidence of age.

Most dermatologists agree there's little any product can do to turn back the clock. The key to a smooth complexion, they say, lies in damage limitation and sadly, that means staying out of the sun.

Cleansing

◆ Gently cleanse your face once a day before you go to sleep. Twice a day is overdoing it. Overstripping can actually lead to increased oil production and spots. If you prefer to use soap and water, then do.

◆ Be gentle. Some therapists recommend exfoliating with scrubs or rough sponges to remove the top layer of dead cells and expose new fresh cells underneath. But in reality caution is required. Remember your skin can be as little as 0.1mm thin (eyelids have the thinnest skin), so it doesn't take much to get rid of a few dead cells.

◆ Over-vigorous exfoliation can remove the skin's first line of defence against radiation, leaving it more sensitive to sun damage and the ageing effects of UV light. It can also lead to tiny broken veins, redness, dryness and irritation.

◆ Gentle exfoliation is probably best achieved with one of the new alpha hydroxy acid formulations, which exfoliate by increasing cell turnover.

Moisturizing

As your skin ages, moisturizers can help the skin look smooth and well conditioned. When you are young your skin may not need moisturizer, although sun protection is a must. Skipping moisturizer won't increase your risk of wrinkles.

◆ Pick a moisturizer to suit your skin type. If your skin is oily avoid using ingredients with a high oil content.

◆ Don't use too much. Your skin can only absorb so much: more isn't better. Your skin will expel excess moisturiser, but too much can lead to blocked pores or acne.

◆ Many dermatologists rate humidifiers above day and night creams to keep the skin moisturized. A pan of water next to the radiator can help compensate for the drying effects of central heating.

▽ *Be gentle with your skin. Wash with soap and water and avoid over-vigorous exfoliation. A good moisturizing cream applied to your face and body will help to smooth your skin.*

△ *Choose a moisturizer that suits your skin type and don't use too much, as your skin can only absorb a limited amount. Excess moisturizer can also lead to blocked pores.*

Sun care protection

Day-long protection from the assault of UV rays will protect your skin from the ageing effects of the sun and from skin cancer too. Guarding against tomorrow's damage may even help undo some of the damage of a sunbaked youth. Just as your lungs can start to repair themselves when you give up smoking, so can the skin make amends when given the chance.

▷ *Always protect your skin from the harmful rays of the sun. Ultraviolet damage builds up whenever you are exposed to the sun and results in premature ageing of the skin and can even cause skin cancer.*

SKIN PROTECTION

◆ Wear sun protection every day. Look for a moisturiser with UV protection. UV damage is cumulative and adds up when you are out shopping, walking the dog, or playing tennis, not just when you are on the beach sunbathing. You don't have to get burnt for the ageing effects of the sun to penetrate your skin.

◆ Wear SPF protection of 15 or more. This will shield against the burning caused by UVB rays as well as the ageing effects of deep-penetrating UVA rays. For longer periods outside choose a higher SPF of 20 or more.

◆ Don't sunbathe for hours even wearing a sun cream. Sun creams can't protect you against all the damaging effects of UV. Experts are now concerned that sun screens may give people a false sense of security without fully protecting against skin cancer.

◆ A sunbed tan is not safe either. Although sunbeds are designed not to burn the skin, their UVA rays penetrate deep into the skin causing changes which can lead to wrinkles and even skin cancer.

◆ Check your body regularly for signs of skin cancer such as new growths, or moles that bleed, itch or change shape.

Hands and Nails

Hands are always on show and yet they're among the most neglected parts of the body. We expose them to all sorts of substances we would never consider putting on our faces. Would you consider splashing your cheeks with boiling water and washing-up liquid several times a day? I don't think so.

Constantly subjected to washing-up water, detergents and the weather, it's hardly surprising they age so rapidly.

As we get older our nails become more brittle and likely to break. The worst culprit is water, whose drying effects are more damaging than anything else. A study at the University of Arkansas found that repeated wet-dry treatment produced visible peeling within 48 hours. It is thought that the drying out period – which cannot be avoided by towel or hot air drying – dissolves the glue-like substances that hold the nails together. The answer is to get the hands wet as little as possible or wear washing-up gloves.

If you don't like wearing gloves, keep hand lotion by the kitchen sink and smother your hands before you dip them into the hot water.

◆ To avoid the ageing effects of the sun, apply a handcream with UV filters or sun screen several times a day.

◆ If your hands are very dry and cracked, soak them in a cup of warm olive oil. Place the bottle of oil in a pan of very hot water for several minutes. Fill a teacup with oil and dip your fingers in for a few minutes. Remove your fingers and massage the oil into your hands.

◆ Protein, vitamins A, B, C and E, zinc, calcium, sulphur and iron will all benefit the nails. Gelatin has often been claimed to improve them, although there is no evidence that it does. Biotin, found in egg whites, may also help strengthen the nails.

Home manicure

◆ File your nails to the desired length. Use the smooth side of the emery board and file from side to centre. Never saw backwards and forwards as this weakens the nail and encourages it to break.

◆ The strongest nails are flat across the top and rounded at the edges.

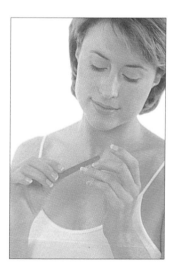

△ *Use the smooth side of an emery board to file your nails to the desired length.*

△ *Gently ease back your cuticles with your fingertips or by using an 'orange' stick.*

△ *Massage your hands and nails with a good handcream or moisturizer.*

◁ Take regular breaks from any repetitive hand movements to avoid painful RSI.

◆ Massage a cuticle cream into the nail area to minimize and moisturize your cuticles.

◆ Never cut your cuticles.

◆ Soak your hands in warm water and almond oil.

◆ Gently ease back your cuticles with your fingertips, then remove any dead skin with a cottonbud dipped in cuticle remover.

◆ Dry your hands thoroughly and massage with a rich handcream.

◆ Squeak nails dry with a little nail-varnish remover, then apply a layer of acetone-free base coat to protect and strengthen the nails.

◆ Apply varnish and finish with a top coat of clear varnish to prevent chipping. Manicurists recommend the three-stroke method – one stroke in the centre then one to each side.

◆ A fresh coat of varnish applied nightly extends your manicure's lifespan.

REPETITIVE STRAIN INJURY

Small repetitive movements such as holding the hands in unnatural positions, can cause crippling pain in the hands and arms known as Repetitive Strain Injury (RSI).

Those most likely to suffer include typists, journalists, hairdressers and musicians. The best way to help is to take regular breaks and do hand exercises.

◆ Clench your fingers tightly into a ball then spread your fingers wide.

◆ Let the hands hang limp and revolve each one slowly from the wrist, in one direction then the other.

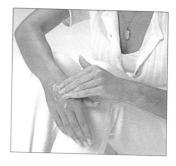

△ To avoid the ageing effects of the sun, apply a handcream with UV filters

△ Dry your nails and apply coloured varnish. Finish with a top coat of clear varnish.

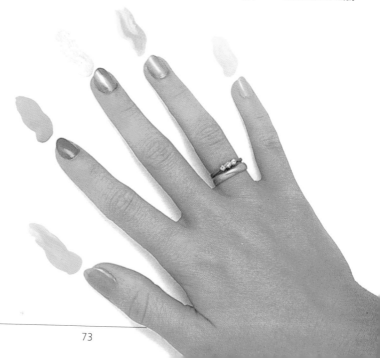

Teeth

*Our teeth are on show every time we smile – so it's vital they are kept
in good condition. Humans develop their first set of teeth in the first
two years of life and then get their adult teeth at around age six.
These teeth have to last us a lifetime, so it makes sense to take
care of them properly.*

△ *Clean your teeth carefully after every
meal and ask your dentist to check that your
brushing technique is correct.*

The good news is that, with current advances in dental care, most people can expect to keep their own teeth well into old age.

Dental care

Good dental care involves regular cleaning and visits to the dentist. Cut down on sugary foods and drinks, to reduce your risk of tooth decay and choose toothpastes

▽ *A winning smile is the result of good
dental hygiene and brushing teeth regularly.*

containing fluoride. Eat plenty of calcium-rich foods and protein, as both are essential for healthy teeth.

Many people do not brush their teeth properly. Ask your dentist for feedback about what parts you are missing: a build-up of tartar is a good guide. The hard up-and-down scrubbing that many people use can actually push the gums back and make receding gums worse. The most widely approved technique involves angling the toothbrush at 45 degrees and wriggling it against the teeth so that the bristles poke between. Count to five then move on. Special attention should be paid to the back teeth and spaces between the teeth and the gumline. Ask your dentist to show you proper brushing technique.

Even careful brushing only gets rid of about fifty per cent of plaque build-up. Plaque is a sticky build-up of bacteria which coats the teeth and can become lodged below the gumline, leading to gum disease and eventually erosion of the bone and loss of the tooth.

The American Dental Association estimates that by 35, three-quarters of all Americans have signs of the disease including inflamed, bleeding or receding gums – though most people are unaware of it. It is only when the teeth become wobbly, an abscess appears or a dentist

finds deep pockets in the gum that the extent of the disease is apparent.

Careful flossing can help get rid of plaque and protect your teeth: do it at least once a day. Wrap the floss around the tooth, slide it down to the gum and back up again. Repeat all round your mouth.

Visit the dental hygienist at least twice a year to have your teeth polished and gums checked for signs of disease.

Bright-Eyes

*Everyone should get their eyes tested regularly, yet most people
ignore this advice because they haven't noticed a problem.
But unless you know what you should be seeing, how can you judge
how good your vision is?*

EYE CARE

◆ Have your eyes tested regularly if
you wear glasses or contact lenses.

◆ Avoid eye strain if you work at a
computer screen or in flickering light.

◆ Eat plenty of vitamin-rich fresh fruit
and vegetables.

Eye tests are important because an optician can detect all sorts of problems besides bad sight. By looking into your eyes an optician can detect conditions such as high blood pressure, high cholesterol and glaucoma long before you notice any symptoms. Glaucoma can cause blindness if it is not caught and treated early.

If you need glasses, have your eyes tested at least every two years in case your prescription changes. Contact lens wearers should see an optician more frequently: at least once a year.

If you work on a computer, avoid eye strain by giving your eyes a break: make a point of focusing on objects different distances away every few minutes. Working in a poor or flickering light will also increase eye strain.

There is some truth to the saying that carrots help you see in the dark. Packed with beta-carotene, they are a rich source of one of the anti-oxidant vitamins eye experts say we need for good eye health. People who eat plenty of fruit and vegetables rich in beta-carotene and vitamins C and E reduce their risk of cataracts, while anorexics with poor vitamin intake suffer from an increased incidence of cataracts.

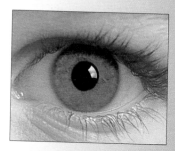

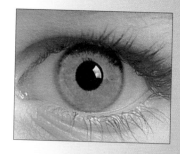

▽ *If you need glasses, have your eyesight
tested at least every two years.*

△ *If you wear contact lenses to correct your
vision you may wish to choose coloured
lenses for special occasions.*

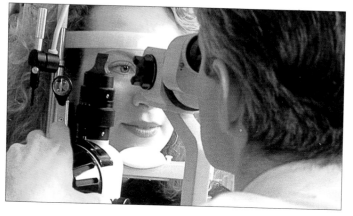

Amazing Feet

Tucked away inside our shoes, feet fall low down our list of priorities when it comes to beauty. In fact, 40 per cent of British women do little more than trim their toenails. The trouble is many women feel that they have ugly feet and would rather ignore them.

We often squash our feet into tight, high-heeled shoes or sweaty trainers and plod around on them all day. Yet there's nothing worse than painful feet, so why not start paying them the attention they deserve? A home pedicure and soothing massage will help to revive aching feet.

Caring for your feet

◆ Dry your feet thoroughly after every shower or bath. Damp skin will encourage fungal infections such as athlete's foot, which flourish in warm, damp environments.

◆ Sprinkle your feet with talcum powder, which will absorb any excess water.

◆ Never buy shoes in the morning, as your feet swell throughout the day.

◆ Never buy shoes that are too small. Try standing on a piece of paper and drawing around your feet. Put your shoes on top of the foot print. Which is larger? If your foot outlines are larger than your shoes then you are probably buying the wrong size or shape for your feet.

◆ Try not to wear the same shoes all day. Walk to work in a comfortable pair of shoes and take another pair to wear at the office.

◆ Don't buy shoes with heels more than 5cm (2in) high. Save high heels for evening wear only. The angle of the shoe throws all your weight onto the delicate bones at the front of your foot. It is actually the thick heel bone which is designed to carry most of your weight.

◆ Soothe swollen feet in a bowl of cold water.

Chiropody

If you have a lot of hard skin on your feet you may need to see a chiropodist, who will remove it using a scalpel. Chiropodists are also trained to deal with ingrown toenails, corns and skin conditions like athlete's foot. They can also give advice on bunions, which can often be helped by an arch support that fits inside the shoe.

Hard skin is the body's way of protecting itself from a build-up of pressure and is often a sign of too-tight shoes. Fallen arches can also cause hard skin but again can be corrected with a proper arch support, which may need to be fitted by a foot specialist known as a podiatrist.

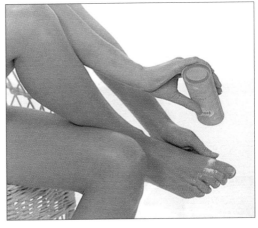

◁ △ *Dry your feet thoroughly, and sprinkle with talcum powder.*

A HOME PEDICURE

A salon pedicure is a wonderful treat, but it's just as easy to get good results at home.

◆ Remove old nail varnish.

◆ Clip your toenails straight across, using clippers. Clippers are easier to use than scissors and less likely to encourage ingrown toenails. Smooth off any rough edges with an emery board. Always file from the outside of the nail towards the centre.

◆ Soak feet in a washing-up bowl of warm water. Add a few drops of lavender essential oil.

◆ Use a pumice stone to remove dead skin.

◆ Dry feet carefully, paying special attention to the area between your toes.

◆ Apply a cuticle remover. Leave for two minutes then gently push back your cuticles using an orange stick wrapped in cotton wool.

◆ Finish with a moisturizing foot massage.

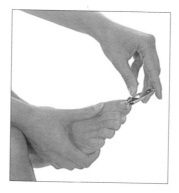
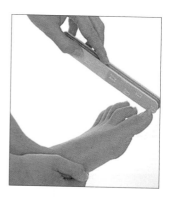

▽ A home pedicure and foot massage will help to revive tired, aching feet.

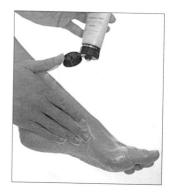

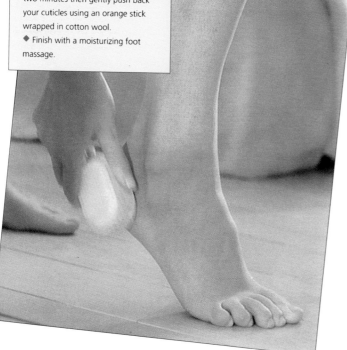

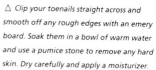

△ Clip your toenails straight across and smooth off any rough edges with an emery board. Soak them in a bowl of warm water and use a pumice stone to remove any hard skin. Dry carefully and apply a moisturizer.

Massage for Relaxation

You don't need to be an expert to realize the healing power of touch. What could be more natural than to rub an aching shoulder or stroke a furrowed brow?

In a study at Harvard Medical School, patients about to have similar operations were divided into two groups. The night before the operation the anaesthetist gave one group the usual talk about procedure, but with the other group he sat on their bed, held their hands and was generally sympathetic. This second group asked for fewer drugs and were on average, dismissed from hospital three days earlier.

Massage is really just an extension of the human instinct to touch or be touched. It can help you relax, improve your circulation, aid digestion and, by stimulating the lymphatic system, speed up the elimination of waste products. Above all a good massage will make you feel pampered and well cared for.

Who can it help?

You don't have to be ill to enjoy a massage and benefits can range from unknotted muscles to soaring energy levels. Once thought of as an indulgence for the idle rich, massage is now finding acceptance by mainstream medicine and is even used in hospitals to help relieve the symptoms of illnesses including cancer and AIDS.

Massage works by relieving knotted muscles and causing the brain to produce endorphins – natural painkillers that create feelings of well-being and contentment. It is particularly helpful for people suffering from high blood pressure, headaches and insomnia. On the most basic level, massage can relieve the back and neck pain caused by a day spent hunched over a desk or computer. The soothing effects also help people who are suffering from stress and anxiety.

Does it work?

There's plenty of evidence that massage really does work. In one study asthmatics who were given upper body massages reported less severe symptoms, probably due to reduced stress levels. Another study found massage afforded breast cancer patients a greater sense of well-being. One study of premature babies found that those given a daily massage gained fifty per cent more weight than a group who weren't massaged, and were ready to leave hospital several days earlier.

The power of touch is so strong it can even counter the effects of powerful poisons. In an experiment, rabbits which were stroked and petted while being fed carcinogens survived, whereas a control group who were given the poison but no contact soon died.

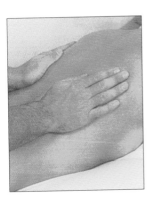

△ Massage the back firmly in wide, circling strokes, starting at the base of the spine.

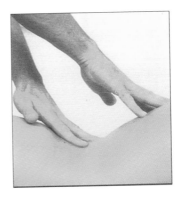

△ Use light, feathering strokes with the fingertips down the length of the back.

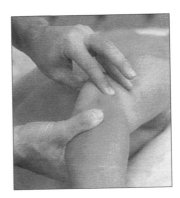

△ Areas of soft muscle can be rolled gently between fingertips and thumb.

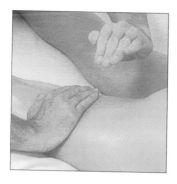

△ *Use both hands for alternate cross-strokes on the legs and upper thighs.*

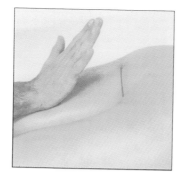

△ *For greater friction, use firm pressure with the heel of your hand on large muscles.*

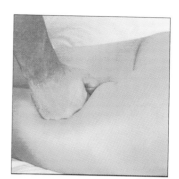

△ *Press your fist firmly into the fleshy areas of the buttocks, using a circular motion.*

Where does it come from?

Massage has been used throughout history, and is something we all do instinctively. In fact massage is probably one of the oldest medical treatments around. Ancient Chinese, Indian and Egyptian manuscripts all refer to the use of massage to cure diseases and heal injuries. In ancient Greek and Roman literature massage was often advocated before and after sport, after bathing or as a medical treatment for digestive problems, melancholia, asthma and even sterility.

A relaxing massage

A back massage will usually last for 30 minutes and a full body massage should last around an hour. There are usually four basic forms: effleurage (stroking), petrissage (or kneading), friction (or pressure), percussion (or drumming).

There's no reason why you shouldn't get a friend or partner to massage you, or give massages yourself. You don't need to be a trained masseuse to harness your intuitive healing powers. Simply follow these basic principles for a healthy and enjoyable massage:

◆ Work in a warm, draught-free room.

◆ Set the mood by ensuring the lighting is soft – candlelight is perfect – and play relaxing 'new age' or classical music.

◆ Use a firm, comfortable surface such as a carpeted floor.

◆ Maintain a firm, regular rhythm with your hand movements flowing one into the next.

◆ Don't use anything but pure vegetable or baby oil. Mineral and unrefined oils will clog the pores.

◆ Warm the oil first in your hands – a teaspoon should be enough – don't pour it directly onto your partner's body.

◆ After you have massaged one area cover it with a blanket or towel to keep the muscles warm.

◆ Make sure your partner wraps up warmly after the massage.

Shiatsu

This is an increasingly popular form of massage, which uses pressure to stimulate the body's energy channels – a network of paths carrying vital energy around the body, according to Chinese and Japanese tradition. The practitioner uses his body weight applied through the heel of the hand, elbows, knees and feet.

◁ *Treat yourself to a professional massage.*

Aromatherapy

Aromatherapy uses highly concentrated plant oils or essences to treat illnesses and influence mood. These essences – also known as essential oils – are highly scented and are believed to have medicinal properties and natural healing powers. Aromatherapy can also have a powerful effect on your mood and emotions as well, using smell both to relax and invigorate.

△ *The scent of flowers is naturally relaxing and has a calming effect.*
▽ *The fragrantly scented oils used in aromatherapy can be inhaled, vaporized in facial steams or used for massage.*

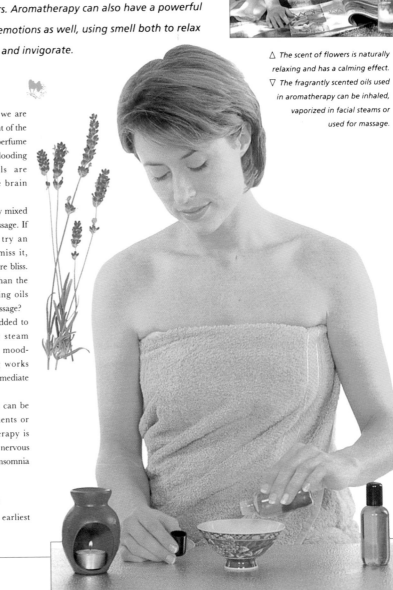

We don't realize how strongly we are affected by scents, but the scent of the sea or the smell of your mother's perfume can bring all sorts of memories flooding back. This is because smells are interpreted by the area of the brain responsible for emotions.

The pure plant oils are usually mixed with vegetable oil and used in massage. If you ever have the chance to try an aromatherapy massage don't miss it, because this treatment is really pure bliss. What could be more heavenly than the relaxing aroma of sweet smelling oils combined with a stress-defying massage?

Undiluted oils can also be added to baths, used in compresses or steam inhalations, or burnt to give a mood-enhancing perfume. Inhaling works quickest because smell has an immediate effect on the brain.

The aromatic plant essences can be used in healing, beauty treatments or simply for pleasure. Aromatherapy is especially good for stress-related nervous conditions such as headaches or insomnia or recurring illnesses.

Where does it come from?

Aromatherapy was used in the earliest

△ *The pure plant essences are usually mixed with vegetable oil and used in massage.*

△ *Aromatherapy combines the relaxation of massage with the stimulating power of smell.*

DO-IT-YOURSELF MASSAGE

Leading aromatherapist Maggie Tisserand recommends the following remedies in her book *Aromatherapy For Women*.

◆ Depression or period pains: clary sage.

◆ Travel sickness: lavender or peppermint.

◆ Mental fatigue: basil, rosemary, rosewood or lemongrass.

◆ Insomnia: lavender.

◆ Revitalizing pep-me-up: rosemary and rosewood; or rosemary and geranium; or rosemary and bergamot.

◆ Premenstrual tension: clary sage, lavender and ylang-ylang.

civilizations of Egypt, India, China and Mesopotamia. French chemist Professor Rene Gattefosse pioneered their use in modern medicine when he discovered the healing power of lavender.

On burning his hand, he plunged it into it a nearby jar of lavender oil and found the burn miraculously healed without any blisters or scars. He went on to use essential oils during the First World War to treat wounded soldiers. Then in the middle of the twentieth century Austrian biochemist and beautician Marguerite Maury developed the modern approach to aromatherapy using essential oils in her beauty and skin treatments.

Is it safe?

Practitioners believe aromatherapy is generally free from side-effects and many can even be used to treat young babies. But despite their sweet innocuous smell, essential oils must still be used with caution. They should not be taken internally unless diluted and then only under the supervision of a medically qualified practitioner. A whole list of them

should not be used during pregnancy as they may cause miscarriage: pregnant women should check carefully before using any. Some oils can cause irritation or even severe burning if put onto the skin undiluted.

What doctors think

Many medical doctors are becoming aware of the benefits of aromatherapy and treatment is beginning to be offered in some hospitals. Research shows that the oils can be absorbed through the skin – possibly through sweat glands or hair follicles – or through inhalation, but beyond that little is known as to how aromatherapy actually works.

Although research at Yale University has found that various odours can lower blood pressure: the smell of spiced apples was particularly effective. Other research has shown pleasant smells can reduce pain.

Using the oils

Add six to eight drops to a hot bath (do not add until the bath is full: adding oils under running taps reduces their potency

as they have a tendency to evaporate). Put 10 drops onto a handkerchief and inhale. Or make a compress by adding eight or 10 drops to half a cup of water and soaking a piece of folded cotton wool in it; then wring out the water and apply.

To make a massage oil, mix three drops of essential oil with 50ml (2fl oz) of carrier oil. Use a more diluted blend for your face.

△ *A few drops of essential oil in a bowl of hot water will release an energizing vapour.*

Yoga

Yoga may appeal to you if you like the idea of exercise which addresses not only your body, but also your mind and spirit. Many people think of yoga as an easy exercise option but it is deceptively tough, requiring not only strength and stamina but enormous concentration.

Yoga works on many levels and the level you enter into is up to you. You can use it as an exercise to stretch out tense muscles and build strength, or to let go of worries and breath energy into your body. Yoga also gives you an internal workout by massaging your liver, lungs, kidneys, spleen and heart.

But yoga is not just concerned with exercise; it can be a spiritual path. True yoga devotees adopt a way of living which is peaceful and harmonious, devoted to simplicity and cleanliness and which rejects greed or anything which harms other creatures. Not that you have to aim for guru status in order to benefit from yoga healthwise.

Yoga assumes there is a basic link between the mind and body and that one cannot be affected without the other. In other forms of exercise you can allow your mind to wander, but in yoga your mind is focused on your breathing and the posture. As you become more practiced this brings about a sense of mental and physical balance and harmony, not to mention fantastic stress-busting benefits.

There are several schools of yoga. The form we are most familiar with in the West is Hatha yoga which uses the physical postures, or asanas, such as shoulder stands and the lotus position. There are several other forms which are just as important: Raja (which focuses on

△ *The half lotus is an easy position to adopt for meditation. Keep your head, neck and spine straight, and legs crossed as a firm base.*

mind control); Karma (moral action); Jnana (intellect and understanding) and Bakti (a devotional aspect).

What are the health benefits?

The goal of yoga is to harness the body's vital energy, known as prana, and direct it in positive healing ways. Women who

THE MOUNTAIN

△ *Sit with your legs crossed in front of you and your hands resting over your knees.*

△ *As you breathe in, slowly raise your arms in wide arcs, to meet above your head.*

△ *Stretch upwards with your palms together. Breathe out as you bring your arms down.*

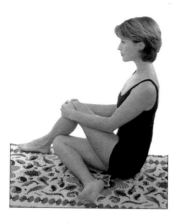

△ Bring your right heel up to your left buttock and cross your left leg over the right.

△ Raise your right arm, and using your left arm for balance, twist your upper body right.

△ Twist your body and head as far as you can with comfort and hold for a few moments.

practice regular yoga say it has helped them with all sorts of health problems, offering relief from headaches, backache, asthma, sinusitis, insomnia and constipation.

Yoga can also help improve posture, flexibility, strength and circulation. Some devotees say it not only brings good health but also energy, beauty and poise.

Where does it come from?

Yoga originated in ancient India and was handed down by teachers to their students as secret teachings which were regarded as divine. It wasn't until about 300BC that the important yoga teacher Patanjali drew up a written classification of the discipline. These Yoga Sutras are a series of disciplines that are designed to purify both the body and mind in a natural progression, and which lead the yogi to a state of enlightenment.

IS IT SAFE?

◆ If performed incorrectly some of the yoga postures could put undue stress on your back, so it is best to start under the guidance of a qualified teacher.

◆ Move slowly and smoothly in and out of each posture and never push your body beyond the point where it is ready to go.

◆ Do not bounce or stretch to the point of strain.

◆ Inhale and exhale through your nose. Imagine you are breathing energy into the muscles you are stretching.

HEAD TO KNEE

△ Sit with one leg straight in front of you and the other bent with heel to thigh.

△ Stretch your arms up above your head with your palms together as you breathe in.

△ Breathe out as you bend forward fully, to clasp your extended foot with both hands.

Homeopathy

Homeopathy is a complementary medicine which aims to treat the whole person by boosting the body's natural healing ability. Homeopathy is based on the principle of treating like with like. So illnesses are treated with substances which would cause the symptoms of the illness in a healthy person.

△ *Homeopathy is based on 'like cures like'.*

In homeopathy, maintaining a healthy lifestyle, coping with stress and adopting a healthy, emotional outlook all play an important part in the prevention of illness.

Homeopaths aim to resolve imbalance rather than just dealing with the symptoms. To achieve this balance they use remedies made from a diverse range of plant, mineral and animal substances,

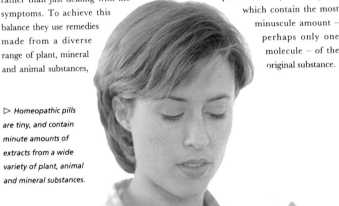

▷ *Homeopathic pills are tiny, and contain minute amounts of extracts from a wide variety of plant, animal and mineral substances.*

from common foods such as honey, to toxic substances such as snake venom.

The substances are highly diluted and the remedies are said to be more effective the more diluted they are. Homeopaths prescribe tiny white pills, which contain the most minuscule amount – perhaps only one molecule – of the original substance.

Homeopaths treat not only the disease but the whole person, taking into account the patient's constitutional type, their likes and dislikes and emotional state as well as their symptoms. So five patients with the same symptoms might all receive different prescriptions.

How did it begin?

The origins of homeopathy date back to 1810 when the German medical doctor Samuel Hahnemann first proposed it as an alternative to the medicine of the day. Hahnemann was disillusioned with harsh treatments such as bloodletting and purging, which he believed often did more harm than good. His new approach was based on gentle, balanced remedies which encouraged the body to cure itself.

His system of medicine was inspired by the discovery that a herbal remedy for malaria, cinchona tree bark, actually caused the symptoms of the disease (cinchona contains quinine, the first drug used against malaria).

Hahnemann spent many years experimenting on himself and his followers, testing various substances and recording the symptoms they produced. Subsequently, patients suffering similar symptoms were treated with these substances, usually with encouraging results.

Side effects?

Homeopathic remedies are diluted so many thousands of times that even substances which would normally be harmful are rendered safe. Symptoms may get slightly worse before they improve. This is known as a 'healing crisis'.

What doctors think

Many doctors find it hard to believe that homeopathic solutions which are so weak can have any effect at all. Orthodox medical doctors believe that any benefits produced by homeopathy are almost certainly psychological: you believe the remedies will help and so they do, rather than because they really have any effect on their own. However, there have been a number of studies on animals and children where relief from symptoms are difficult to explain purely on the grounds of wishful thinking.

◁ Red Foxglove (Digitalis purpurea) is used in remedies to regulate the heartbeat.

◁The roots of the Blue Flag (Iris versicolor) are used to make a homeopathic remedy that is prescribed for a number of specific symptoms, including the control of pain.

Reflexology

Reflexology is an ancient form of pressure point therapy which focuses on the soles of the feet. As with many other complementary healing techniques, illnesses are thought to occur when energy channels are blocked.

DO-IT-YOURSELF REFLEXOLOGY

◆ Headaches – massage the tips of your big toes and their outer sides.

◆ Neck ache – massage the base of the big toes.

◆ Back ache – massage the spine reflexes along the inside edge of each foot.

◆ Colds or hay fever – massage the sinus reflex found at the back and sides of the smaller toes.

Reflexology is one of a family of zone therapies which rely on the principle that applying pressure on one part of the body can cause a change in another part. Tender spots on the feet are thought to reflect a problem in the corresponding body part. Healing takes place by applying pressure to the appropriate area and so 'unblocking' the energy.

Reflexologists use your feet as a guidebook to your whole body. They claim to be able to detect both current and past problems in different zones of the body such as the neck, kidneys, back and reproductive system. The right foot is said to reflect the right side of the body and the left foot, the left side of the body.

Reflexology is used for a wide range of conditions including back pain, migraine, digestive problems, period pains, sinus problems and stress. Some people believe it has helped them deal with multiple sclerosis, heart problems and strokes.

Reflexologists say they can spot early warning signs and treat the illness before it emerges or, when appropriate, recommend their client sees a medical specialist.

Most people find the treatment very relaxing and, despite what you might expect, it doesn't usually tickle.

Origins

Reflexology is thought to have originated in China some 5,000 years ago. It was also used by the ancient Egyptians and in India and Japan. In 1913 an ear, nose and throat specialist, Dr William Fitzgerald, introduced 'zone therapy' to the West.

His ideas were later taken up by his assistant Eunice Ingham who organized the therapy into its modern form, lecturing all over the United States of America and writing several books.

Is it safe?

Reflexology is not suitable for pregnant women, people with osteoporosis (brittle bones), thrombosis, arthritis in the feet, thinning veins or phlebitis (blood clots).

What do doctors think?

Although there's no controlled research to show that reflexology works, most doctors accept that little harm can come from a foot massage and that it should at least be therapeutic, in that most people find the treatment quite soothing.

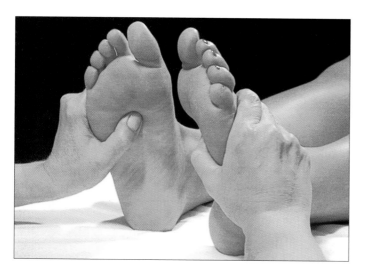

◁ *Reflexologists use your feet to build up a picture of the health of your whole body.*

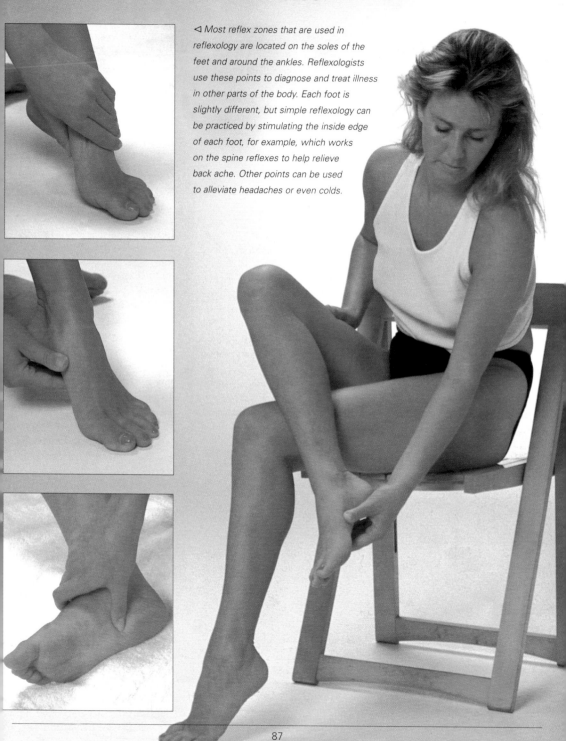

◁ Most reflex zones that are used in reflexology are located on the soles of the feet and around the ankles. Reflexologists use these points to diagnose and treat illness in other parts of the body. Each foot is slightly different, but simple reflexology can be practiced by stimulating the inside edge of each foot, for example, which works on the spine reflexes to help relieve back ache. Other points can be used to alleviate headaches or even colds.

Back to Basics

Most back pain is the result of muscular tension brought about by poor posture, bad seating or bending and lifting incorrectly. The way we stand, sit and use our bodies can have a considerable influence on our backs. Slouching in front of the television as a child and teenager may not cause us problems when we are young, but anything which leads to poor alignment of the spine sets the foundations for problems in later life.

Our postural habits develop over many years and usually have their roots in childhood, when we copy our parents or other adults close to us. There are all sorts of odd and quirky variations on posture but, according to osteopath Roger Newman Turner, on the whole people can be divided into slouchers and thrusters.

The sloucher rounds her shoulders and pushes her chin forward and down while her abdominal muscles sag. The opposite is true of the thruster who pushes out both her chin and chest like a ballet dancer.

According to alternative practitioners, poor posture not only leads to back pain, but can influence our health in a much broader way. For example, the sloucher's shallow breathing and concave chest can cause chest problems, while her weak sagging abdomen can cause gynaecological problems and constipation.

On the other hand, the thruster may suffer from headaches, dizziness, throat problems, chest disorders, breathing irregularities, hernia and bladder problems.

▷ *Practitioners of the Alexander Technique teach their clients to retrain their posture.*

Good posture

What do we mean by good posture? First of all we can say that good posture isn't the army-style stance – shoulders back and stomach in – which is probably worse than any slouch we've developed on our own. Rather, perfect posture occurs when our muscles, ligaments and tendons are doing the minimum amount of work necessary and no more.

Practitioners of the Alexander Technique teach their clients to leave behind lifelong patterns of misuse, to resist the familiar and instead use their bodies as nature intended. Other movement therapies such as t'ai chi and yoga also aim to free the body's energy stores which are locked into tight muscles and stiffening joints.

Taking care of your back

◆ Walk tall: imagine there is a piece of string attached to the top of your head pulling you upwards and forwards.

◆ Your weight should rest on the balls of your feet.

◆ Always bend from your knees, not your waist. Bending from the waist puts extreme pressure on the discs in your lower spine, especially if you are picking something up.

◆ Split heavy shopping into two bags and carry in both hands so that your body is balanced. Try to use trolleys and suitcases with wheels rather than struggle with heavy bags.

◆ On long car journeys, stop and stretch your legs every couple of hours.

◆ Your office chair should allow you to sit with your knees slightly lower than your hips.

◆ If you work at a VDU make sure the screen is at eye level. This may mean piling books under the screen to bring it up to the correct height.

◆ Get up and walk around every couple of hours.

◆ If you wake up with backache, check your bed. Avoid very soft, sagging

mattresses. A good bed should support the body evenly and be easy to move about on. Beds that are too hard aren't good either as they tend to iron out the natural curves in your spine.

◆ Don't cradle the phone under your chin to free your hands as this causes neck strain.

◆ Kneel down to do gardening instead of bending, and avoid too much digging.

◆ Kneel rather than bend when cleaning the bath or floor.

◆ Avoid wearing high heels too often.

If you do get a bad back:

Try to stay active rather than retiring to bed. In fact, staying in bed for more than two days is probably the worst thing you can do, because bed rest leads to bone loss and general weakness. Muscle weakness is often the cause of back pain.

Rather than stay in bed, exercise may be the best thing you can do. Several studies have shown that people who exercise with a bad back recover faster than their sedentary counterparts. The best exercises are low-impact activities which do not stress the back, such as swimming (preferably not breast stroke), cycling and walking. Strengthening the abdominal muscles also helps by taking pressure off your spine.

Just remember to warm up before you start and never do any exercise that makes your back hurt more. It's also best to avoid exercise involving sudden or twisting movements like tennis and squash.

◁ *Simple yoga positions are useful for strengthening abdominal muscles and keeping the spine flexible. Try sitting with the soles of your feet held together with your hands. Keeping your knees as close to the floor as you can, stretch your upper body forwards towards the floor. Hold this position for a few moments, then relax.*

Acupuncture

Acupuncture is an ancient Chinese therapy which uses needles to treat health problems. In acupuncture, therapy is aimed at detecting any imbalance and restoring it by inserting needles at points along the body's energy channels or 'meridians'.

The therapy works on the basis that illnesses occur when the body's energy flow or *qi* (pronounced 'chee') is knocked off balance. Stimulating the correct point is thought to unblock the energy and allow it to flow freely again.

Any number of things are thought to disrupt *qi*, including emotional upsets, weather conditions, over-eating or under-eating, drug-taking, infections, shock or trauma. Acupuncture aims to get energy flowing again and restore the balance of emotional, physical, mental and spiritual aspects – especially the balance between yin (passive) and yang (stimulating) energy.

Any number of needles can be used, although in practice this usually varies from one to 15 and more experienced practitioners tend to use fewer needles. The patient should start to see results after six to eight sessions. If not, it is unlikely that acupuncture will help.

Acupuncture is particularly well suited to dealing with pain caused by back problems, arthritis and rheumatism, as well as with stress and addictions such as smoking. It has also been found to help people suffering from allergies, angina, anxiety, bronchitis, ulcers, digestive problems and insomnia.

Is it safe?

It is essential to choose a qualified practitioner. These days an acupuncturist must use disposable needles from sealed, sterilized packs. Since disposable needles should always be used there is little risk of infection or HIV.

Acupuncture should be a quick, blood-free and relatively painless procedure. Some people report a slight numbness or tingling at each needlepoint and a feeling of deep relaxation. Most acupuncturists tap the needles just under the skin, although some Chinese practitioners make deeper insertions of up to three or four inches into the body.

What doctors think

A number of studies have found that acupuncture causes the brain to release endorphins, which are the body's natural painkilling chemicals, and that the amount of pain relief experienced after acupuncture is directly linked to the amount of endorphins released.

Other studies have shown that by stimulating nerves it is possible to stop pain signals reaching the brain and it is thought that acupuncture may work in a similar way.

There is also plenty of medical evidence to suggest that acupuncture points are important. They can even be detected electronically, because acupuncture points have lower electrical resistance than the surrounding skin.

◁ *Chinese practitioners often use a combination of deeply inserted needles and heat to relieve specific ailments.*
▷ *Sterilized, disposable acupuncture needles should always be used, so that there is no risk of infection or HIV.*

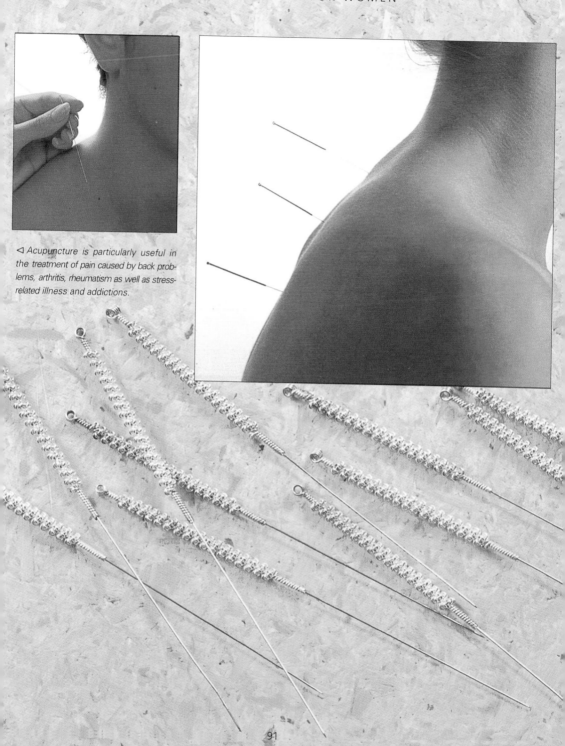

◁ Acupuncture is particularly useful in the treatment of pain caused by back problems, arthritis, rheumatism as well as stress-related illness and addictions.

Manipulative Therapies

Knotted muscles, poor posture and gravity all contribute to back pain and general ill health. But help is at hand in the form of manipulative therapies which can restore health and harmony by correcting problem joints.

Osteopathy

Osteopathy uses manipulation of the body to correct musculo-skeletal problems. Osteopaths believe that misalignment of the skeleton is responsible for pain, discomfort and major as well as minor health problems. They use their hands to massage and manipulate the joints and pay special attention to the vertebrae and spinal discs.

Osteopathy is particularly useful for treatment of neck and back pain although it can also help sports injuries, tension headaches, asthma, bronchitis, period pains, discomforts of pregnancy, migraine and gastrointestinal problems.

Origins

An American doctor called Andrew Taylor Still founded osteopathy in the 1870s, following his dissatisfaction with the orthodox treatments of the day. He combined his detailed knowledge of the human body with research into engineering and came to view the body as a machine. If one part of the machine did not work effectively, he reasoned, nor would the rest. Manipulation, he believed, could restore balance and cure illnesses.

Is it safe?

Osteopathy is not suitable for any one who doesn't like the idea of being cracked and crunched and should only ever be practiced by a fully qualified practitioner.

What doctors think

One of the first complementary therapies to be truly embraced by the medical establishment, osteopathy is now accepted by most doctors as a useful way to treat skeletal problems. Many doctors even refer their patients to osteopaths for skeletal problems, although they would still dispute the use of osteopathy for non-mechanical problems.

Chiropractic

Chiropractic is similar to osteopathy in many ways, since chiropractors also use their hands to manipulate the joints, particularly of the neck and spine. But they rely more than osteopaths on orthodox diagnostic techniques such as X-rays. As well as joint manipulation a chiropractor sometimes applies heat, ice treatment or ultra-sound.

Ninety per cent of chiropractors' patients have some sort of musculo-skeletal problem, particularly neck or back pain. Problems in the back may also cause referred pain in other parts of the

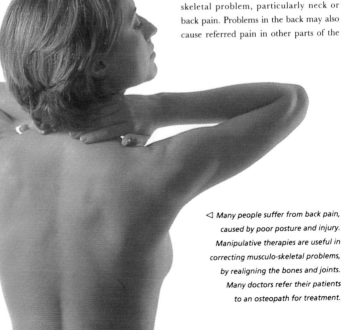

◁ *Many people suffer from back pain, caused by poor posture and injury. Manipulative therapies are useful in correcting musculo-skeletal problems, by realigning the bones and joints. Many doctors refer their patients to an osteopath for treatment.*

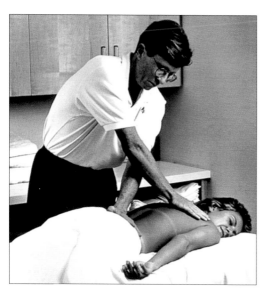

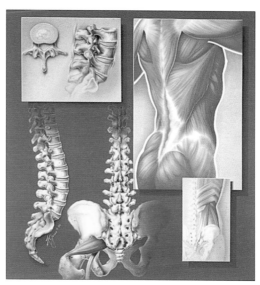

body, since a misplaced bone may press on nerves and disrupt their functioning. Chiropractic is also useful for whiplash injuries and tension headaches. Chiropractors may even discover injuries that have stemmed from childhood falls or were sustained during birth.

Sometimes relief is immediate; other problems may need three or four treatments before the benefits are felt.

Origins

Chiropractic was developed by a healer, Daniel David Palmer, who founded the Palmer School of Chiropractic. In 1895 Palmer treated his office janitor for deafness which had come on suddenly after the man felt a click in his back when bending down. Palmer found some misplaced bones in the man's back, manipulated these and the man's hearing was restored.

What doctors think

Like osteopathy, chiropractic is now well accepted by most orthodox doctors as a

useful method of treating musculo-skeletal problems. The Medical Research Council in the UK even found that chiropractic was 70 per cent more effective than conventional treatments for back pain.

△ Osteopaths are trained to have a detailed knowledge of the human body and can manipulate the skeleton with great precision.
▽ Always ensure that you consult a fully qualified osteopath or chiropractor.

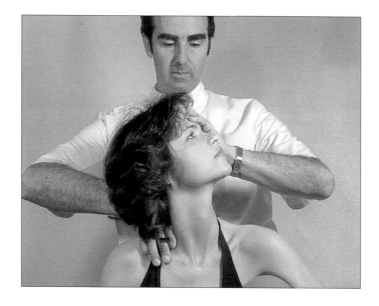

Herbal Remedies

Herbal medicine is still the most widely practiced form of medicine in the world today and even conventional medicine derives many of its drugs from refined plant extracts.

Herbalists take a holistic approach: they consider the individual's needs and strengths before making a prescription to enhance the body's natural healing powers.

Herbalists say their medicine can be of benefit to most people with any illness, although they may also refer patients on to other therapists, such as a chiropractor or osteopath.

Origins

Herbal remedies have been used throughout history, all over the world. The Egyptians, ancient Romans and Greeks all practiced forms of herbal medicine. The Chinese and the Indian cultures also have a long tradition of herbal cures. Even today, in China, herbalism is widely used.

Britain, too, has a long tradition of herbalism: the Druids are believed to have used herbal remedies mixed with mysticism and, from the Dark Ages to medieval times, monasteries kept hand-written records of herbal cures.

Is it safe?

Many people believe that herbal medicine is safer and more natural than the refined ingredients of modern drugs. However, just because it's 'natural' doesn't mean it is harmless. Some herbal remedies are extremely potent and so should only be used following the directions of a qualified herbalist. On the whole however, herbal medicine appears to produce fewer side-effects.

What doctors say

Orthodox medical practitioners recognize that herbal cures were the forerunner of modern medicine. It's certainly true that powerful drugs are derived from plants – 15 per cent of all GPs' prescriptions are plant-based.

Do-it-yourself

You can gain some of the benefits of herbs by incorporating them into your diet. Herbs add extra vitamins and flavour to your food. They will also help you cut down on salt – an extra health bonus.

Making herbal tea

Add boiling water to a teaspoonful of herbs in a cup and leave to steep for three minutes. Strain, and add a little honey to the tea to sweeten it if desired, then drink. Infusions for a gargle should be left to steep for 15 minutes in a teapot, strained and allowed to cool before use.

◁ *Herbs have been grown for many centuries.*
▷ *Add boiling water to a teaspoonful of herbs in a cup to make a potent herbal tea.*

USEFUL HERBS FOR HEALTH

◆ Basil aids digestion and stomach cramps.

◆ Camomile aids relaxation and digestion.

◆ Chives stimulate the appetite; help fight infections and aid recovery after illness.

◆ Fennel is good for curing insomnia, indigestion and nausea.

◆ Garlic helps fight viral infections – particularly those affecting the digestive or respiratory system. Good for colds and heart health.

◆ Mint alleviates wind, constipation, insomnia, vomiting and nausea.

◆ Rosemary is a useful tea for headaches and colds.

◆ Sage makes a good antiseptic lotion for wounds. Sage tea helps relieve anxiety, depression and indigestion.

◆ Thyme makes an antiseptic gargle for coughs and catarrh.

△ Basil

△ Camomile

△ Chives

△ Fennel

△ Ginger Mint

△ Pineapple Mint

△ Rosemary

△ Purple Sage

△ Common Thyme

▷ *Traditional herbal remedies are usually safer and more natural than many modern drugs.*

Index

adrenalin *6*

AIDS *56, 57*

alcohol *8, 24, 58*

anorexia *26, 50, 64*

anti-oxidant *66, 74*

aromatherapy *30, 80*

body image *34, 36, 64*

body fat *8, 16, 34, 38, 42*

breathing *30, 44, 82, 88*

caffeine *30, 60*

calcium *8, 22, 24, 72, 74*

calories *8, 22, 24, 72, 74*

cancer *6, 12, 16, 26, 66, 70, 70*

carbohydrate *8, 16, 20*

chiropodist *76*

condoms *52, 56*

dieting *16, 22, 58,66*

energy *8, 20, 36, 62*

fat *6, 8, 16, 20, 24, 42, 44, 60, 66*

feet *46, 86, 88, 90*

fibre *12, 58*

flexibility *32, 82*

folic acid *24, 58*

health club *32, 42, 48*

herpes *56*

hormones *30, 34, 52, 54, 58, 60, 62*

injury *36, 40, 74*

interval training *40, 42*

jogging *6, 38, 40*

metabolism *16, 34, 62*

muscles *34, 36, 42, 44, 66, 78, 82, 88*

oil *8, 24, 26, 52, 62, 70, 78, 80*

osteopathy *92*

posture *36, 40, 58, 82, 88*

pregnancy *24, 32, 52, 54, 58, 92*

progesterone *60*

protein *8, 26, 68, 72, 74*

pulse *12, 36*

self-esteem *16*

smoking *6, 22, 24, 52, 58, 60, 70, 90*

strength *28, 32, 34, 36, 44, 58, 66, 72, 82, 88, 94*

stress *6, 30, 36, 38, 40, 60, 68, 80, 82, 84, 86, 90*

vegetables *6, 8, 12, 24, 26, 60, 66, 68, 68, 74*

vitamin *8, 12, 24, 26, 60, 66, 68, 74*

water *8, 12, 44, 58, 60, 70, 72, 76, 94*

weight *8, 16, 28, 32, 34, 36, 38, 40, 44, 48, 52, 60, 62, 64, 66, 76, 78, 88*